Surfing the Cryptocurrency Wave

Decoding the Next Generation of Money

Shubhasish Das

ATLANTIC
PUBLISHERS & DISTRIBUTORS (P) LTD

ATLANTIC
PUBLISHERS & DISTRIBUTORS (P) LTD
7/22, Ansari Road, Darya Ganj, New Delhi
Tel.: +91-11-4077 5252, 2327 3880
E-mail: orders@atlanticbooks.com
Web: www.atlanticbooks.com

Published by Atlantic Publishers & Distributors (P) Ltd 2024

Previously Published by SAGE Publications in 2022

Printed & bound in India by Atlantic Print Services

Advance Praise

'Shubhasish has captured the colossal wave of cryptos, triggered by Nakamoto's Bitcoin, and intensified by thousands of altcoins which had followed. Since its birth in 2009, Bitcoin has shifted tectonic plates in the financial world. I would recommend this book to anyone who wants to know the link between money, bitcoin, altcoins, NFTs and blockchain.'

—**Sreeraman Natarajan**, Head,
Finance Transformation and Innovation, British Petroleum

'Fascinating. Honest. Useful. The experience conveyed through this book is invaluable. Knowledge is not enough if you do not turn it into practice, which you will want to start by the time you read the last page of this book.'

—**Lyubomir Atanasov**, CEO and Founder,
European Digital Experts Association (EURODEA)

Dedication

If I have seen further, it is by standing on the shoulders of giants.

—Sir Isaac Newton

Dedicated to the giants of past, present and future.

Contents

Part 3: Bitcoin

Part 4: Crypto World

Preface

There are hundreds of books on cryptocurrencies. Some of them are purely technical and therefore not suitable for laypeople. Others are too simple, providing no value addition. This book attempts to fill this void by putting together all that you need to know about this latest medium of monetary exchange which has taken the world by storm. The book employs analogies and metaphors abundantly to drive home the real crux of the subject while keeping the narrative interesting.

Cryptocurrencies are the culmination of thousands of years of human experience. They carry ideas from economics, computer science, finance, accounting, politics, etc. While their multidisciplinary nature makes them interesting to learn, at the same time, it makes them tedious to grasp. In writing a book on the topic, the main challenge is to link, order and elucidate various concepts for general readers without diluting their essence.

WHO IS THIS BOOK FOR?

This book is for students, professors, corporate executives, MBAs, professionals, lawmakers, entrepreneurs, homemakers and anyone who wants to acquire a solid understanding of cryptocurrencies within a short period. If you have a high-school education, know how to switch on a laptop and watch YouTube on mobile, you should be able to comprehend every word and arm yourself with professional knowledge of cryptocurrencies.

WHAT TO EXPECT FROM THIS BOOK?

It provides a crisp, clear and direct explanation of concepts. Irrelevant discussion is avoided. Complex topics from computer science and economics which are essential for mastering the subject are simplified and included. Myriad questions related to bitcoin, mining, blockchain and other confusing aspects of cryptos are answered. It provides 'concept notes' which reveal crucial aspects of cryptocurrencies and blockchain. The cryptography chapters also have *demos* which you can practise online for free. Understanding money, monetary systems and the role of cryptocurrencies within the system can be exhausting. *The money model* (TMM), which is discussed in Chapter 2, provides a simple framework to understand conventional as well as new forms of money like cryptocurrencies. It also maps out the whole spectrum of digital currencies in a logical tree, which will help readers grasp the breadth of this field in minutes. *Central bank digital currency* or CBDC was the buzzword in 2021. There is a lot of confusion among the general public, bankers and crypto professionals about the structure and implementation of CBDC. This book provides actual case studies of CBDC with various models through which they might be implemented. Finally, it covers all current developments in crypto regulations. However, it is not a cryptocurrency trading book. It doesn't provide investment advice. People who want to create a strong foundation in bitcoin and other cryptocurrencies should read this book. Trading is risky; trading without knowing the thing you are trading is fatal. Only the skilled may ride the cryptocurrency wave; else, horrible consequences may ensue. It is not a coding book either. However, it has enough computer science stuff to help you decide whether you want to become a blockchain and cryptocurrency developer.

HOW TO READ THIS BOOK?

I recommend reading it sequentially. However, readers who are already technically sound may choose to browse specific chapters. The book has 4 parts comprising 27 short chapters.

Part 1 explains cryptocurrencies and how they are linked to traditional money. It starts with money and ends with the introduction to crypto money. It covers a lot of meat in between.

Chapter 1 answers 'What is money?' and 'What are its functions?' Chapter 2 presents a simple model to understand the system of money. Chapter 3 provides a historical background of money from an evolutionary point of view. Chapter 4 elaborates on the problems with present-day money which have forced some of us to think about an alternative. Chapter 5 recounts a few milestones in the historical development of cryptocurrencies. Chapter 6 discusses a technical hurdle which made digital things unsuitable as money. Chapter 7 explains cryptocurrencies using the model described in Chapter 2. This helps the reader to link cryptocurrencies to everything which has been discussed about conventional money. This part ends with Chapters 8 and 9, which demonstrate some essential concepts by creating a hypothetical cryptocurrency.

Part 2 sets the ground for the technical discussion on cryptos. It explains some of the important stuff from cryptography and computer science.

Chapters 10, 11 and 12 are dedicated to a few critical cryptography concepts. Although these chapters are technical, these are the easiest to digest. Chapter 13 dissects the blockchain to its core.

Part 3 is entirely dedicated to bitcoin. It covers almost everything about the world's most valuable cryptocurrency. Concepts learned in previous parts are put into use. Please don't read this part without finishing Part 2. Else, you will miss the insights these chapters offer. Mastering this part will set you apart from amateurs.

Chapter 14 explains bitcoin on five different levels. Chapter 15 provides precise answers to 'What are bitcoins?' 'How do they get killed?' 'Where do bitcoins live?' and 'How are they born?' Chapter 16 describes the bitcoin network and its constituents. Chapter 17 discusses the bitcoin blockchain. Chapter 18 explains how bitcoin works. Everything about bitcoin mining is covered in Chapter 19. Chapter 20 discusses bitcoin from an economic perspective. This part ends with Chapter 21, which answers how bitcoin improvements are made.

Part 4 is a non-technical discussion on alternative coins, tokens, the current regulatory environment, central bank cryptocurrencies, wallets and exchanges. It aims to inform rather than to explain.

Chapter 22 covers the whole spectrum of digital currencies, which helps the reader identify the place of cryptos in digital economy. Various kinds of alternative coins and tokens are discussed in Chapter 23. Critical aspects of Ethereum, world's second-largest cryptocurrency, are covered in Chapter 24. Chapter 25 explains CBDC, which is taking momentum in 2022. Chapter 26 contains a brief discussion of wallets and exchanges which help the reader to buy, sell and store cryptos securely. The book ends with Chapter 27, by discussing the present state of crypto regulations worldwide.

You can send me your feedback and suggestions at mail@shubhasishdas.com.

Disclaimer: All illustrations are created by the author, including some which use licensed icons from flaticons.com.

Acknowledgements

I am grateful to the SAGE team, especially Neha Pal and Manisha Mathews, for their enduring support. I express my gratitude to all my friends and colleagues for bearing the burden of reading the manuscript and providing unbiased feedback. At last, I thank my parents and my beloved wife for their endless tolerance and encouragement, without whom this book wouldn't have been possible.

PART 1
Crypto Money

1 MONEY

The pawn in chess neither has meaning in the sense of representing something, of being sign of something, nor is it just the piece carved out of wood. What the pawn is, is determined by the rules of chess.[1]

What is money is decided by the rules set by a bunch of people, called society. These rules decide what money should or should not do. Imagine browsing through a job portal. Every role tells what the candidate is expected to do. The designation is just a placeholder. It can hold any aspirant who is capable.

Similarly, money is just a role. We expect it to do certain functions. Over the years, we have chosen a variety of things for this role. The diversity of candidates that did this job is epic. It includes cows, seashells, rai stones, tally sticks, gold, silver, cigarettes, mobile minutes, paper notes, gold certificates, bank ledgers and electric pulses in a computer. Therefore, money is what it does. And it does three things: It helps in exchanging, storing and measuring value.[2]

Concept note: Rules are called protocols in computer science. We will use this term often while discussing cryptocurrencies.

1 Wittgenstein, 1984: 150, in Heiner Ganssmann, *Doing Money: Elementary Monetary Theory from a Sociological Standpoint*, 1st edition (Routledge, 2012), 20.

2 N. Gregory Mankiw, '*Money and Inflation*', in *Macroeconomics*, 6th ed (New York: Worth Publishers, 2007), 80–81.

THREE FUNCTIONS OF MONEY

Medium of Exchange

We buy things with it; therefore, it acts as a payment mechanism. It is a tool which facilitates trade and enables the exchange of goods and services. Among the whole spectrum of assets, it is the most liquid. Liquidity is the ability to buy or sell quickly at market price, which makes money the fastest way to settle transactions. For example, Jack brought a car by paying $10,000. The currency USD functioned as a mode of payment in this transaction.

Concept note: Cryptocurrencies are not a widely accepted medium of exchange yet.

Store of Value

Value means the capacity to purchase things. Money stores its ability to buy things over a period. We want its value to stay stable to make our spending decisions with ease. By stability, we mean that the exchange rate between currency and goods stays almost the same in the near future. For example, if 5 coins are required to buy a dozen eggs today, the exchange rate is '5 coins to 12 eggs'. Suppose tomorrow you need 10 coins to get 12 eggs. It means that your currencies *have lost half of their value* as you can buy only six eggs with five coins. We don't experience such wild fluctuation in currency value because the central bank works to keep it stable. Government currencies such as USD and INR act as a good store of purchasing power because of their stability.

Unit of Account

Suppose you had a job interview last week and today you got a call from HR to discuss your salary. You are all excited. Then they said, 'Mr Andy, your monthly salary is 10 cows and 15 wheat bags.' Perplexed, you scratch your head, 'What exactly are 10 cows and 15 bags of wheat worth?' You don't know the exchange rate of cows to wheat, cows to other things or wheat to other things. How many cows does it take to buy a sandwich or onboard a flight? This is where money can help you. It acts as a universal measure of value or a standard unit to price things. Pricing things makes them comparable. It helps you to account and compare your incomes, expenses, properties and obligations. For example, generally, a country's home currency is used as a unit of account. GBP is used to price goods in Great Britain; USD is used in the USA; and CAD is used in Canada.

Concept note: Cryptocurrencies are not stable stores of value, at least not yet. Their value is not managed by a central bank. Instead, price discovery happens in crypto exchanges. Exchanges are online marketplaces, where people go for shopping cryptos. Just like onions and cabbages, prices of cryptocurrencies depend on demand and supply. Since cryptos are comparatively new, and no one has a clear idea about their utility in future, their value fluctuates heavily. Because of this, it is not possible to express the price of goods, services, assets and debts in terms of cryptos. This would require frequent adjustment to the price. Hence, countries and corporates have refrained from using cryptocurrencies as a unit of account. For example, no company prepares its financial statement in terms of bitcoin.

GOOD AND BAD MONEY

Every job has its own skillset. A soldier needs to be courageous, whereas an accountant must be good with numbers. Similarly, there are certain attributes that make a candidate more or less suitable for carrying out the functions of money. Following are *seven properties of good money*.

Scarcity

Good money is scarce in a predictable way. Its supply is never too much, making it a useless store of value; instead, it is available just enough, allowing people to use it as a medium of exchange. For example, seashells could have been good money for a tribal living in deserts but useless for a coastal villager.

Concept note: Digital things are not scarce. Everything stored within your computer, such as images, films, songs and documents, can be copied infinitely. Therefore, digital candidates are unsuitable for performing the role of money. Cryptocurrencies are the first digital candidates in the history of money which could do the job of money without relying on banks and financial institutions.

Fungibility

Good money should be interchangeable or replaceable. For example, a $10 should have the same value as other $10 notes. Governments usually clarify that a torn banknote should have the same value as a fresh note if its serial number is intact.

Concept note: Cryptocurrencies such as bitcoin may not be fungible.

Durability

Good money is strong and durable. You don't want your money to break, erode, deteriorate and disintegrate quickly. For example, metals like gold and silver worked as money for a long time because they could tolerate rough times and last long. At the same time, bananas never took on the role of money because of their perishable nature.

Concept note: Since cryptocurrencies are fully digital, they don't suffer from the durability issues of physical currencies.

Portability and Divisibility

Good money is easy to carry and allows itself to be used in fractions. While these properties are inherent in today's money, it wasn't always the case with ancient currencies.

Example: Portability

Giant rai stones of Yap island did the job of money, but they were far from being portable. Ownership of these stones was passed orally, rather than crushing them into pieces and transporting them to the new owner's home. While chipping them would have made them portable, they would have lost their monetary value. It shows how a currency can be good at one function (store of value) but poor at another (medium of exchange).[3]

Example: Divisibility

Cows did play the role of currencies around 10,000 BCE, but as you can see, they cannot be used in fractions. It was not possible to buy something with a half or quarter cow without destroying its value. However, people found a way to make smaller payments with cows later by fixing the primary unit as a milch cow. For instance, a three-year-old heifer was considered equivalent to half of milch cow, and a yearling heifer meant one-quarter of a milch cow.[4]

Concept note: The digital nature of cryptocurrencies allows them to be highly portable via the Internet. Most of them are divisible into smaller units, making micropayments easy.

Unforgeability

Good money is difficult to forge. No one wants to hold a fake currency. Countries have developed various ways to make their

3 Cora Lee C. Gillilland, *The Stone Money of Yap: A Numismatic Survey.* Smithsonian Studies in History and Technology 23 (Washington, DC: Smithsonian Institution Press, 1975), 75; Jacob Goldstein and David Kestenbaum, 'The Island of Stone Money', NPR, https://www.npr.org/blogs/money/2011/02/15/131934618/the-island-of-stone-money.
4 Isolde ÓBrolcháin Carmody, 'Cows as Currency', Story Archaeology, 22 July 2012, https://storyarchaeology.com/cows-as-currency/#:~:text=One%20unit%20of%20value%20was,as%20a%20unit%20of%20value; Peter Ranscombe, 'A History of Money and How Our Use of It Has Changed down the Centuries', *The Scotsman*, 17 October 2019, https://www.scotsman.com/lifestyle/history-money-and-how-our-use-it-has-changed-down-centuries-1405001

currencies difficult to copy, for example, stamping, inscribing images and shiny tapes, and using invisible symbols which can be seen only using ultraviolet light. Why is forging a problem? Because it breaks the property of scarcity. Forged currencies increase the money supply, thereby decreasing the value of genuine currencies. For example, suppose a pizza costs $10. If we create four copies of $10, we have $50 of currency, but the number of pizzas remains one. As a result, the worth of pizza remains the same, but the value of money decreases. Previously, the pizza required only one $10 bill. Now, it will require five. You could have brought a whole pizza with your authentic $10, but you can only buy one-fifth of pizza because of forged currencies. This is an overly simplistic example of how fake money can create inflation, but you got the idea.

Concept note: Cryptocurrencies are practically impossible to forge as they are created, transacted and protected by heavy cryptography.

Universality

Good money is widely accepted. Most of the government currencies are widely accepted within their home countries. Since USD is a global reserve currency used in international trade, it is accepted almost everywhere globally.

Concept note: Some cryptocurrencies such as bitcoin and Ether are now widely known, providing them a global currency status. However, due to their volatile nature, they are not widely accepted as payments by vendors. But they are truly global as a peer-to-peer (P2P) payment mechanism.

2 MODEL

Money is akin to a job title. In the last chapter, we have understood three functions of this job and the qualities required to become good money. However, whether a candidate can do its job properly depends on the organizational structure, culture, policies and the overall commercial ecosystem. Similarly, we must understand the performance of money in relation to the monetary system. Systems are, by nature, complex, and the monetary system is no exception. Therefore, we will dismantle the monetary system into three rudimentary elements and study their relationships. We will call it the money model (TMM). It will help us map cryptocurrencies back to banknotes, gold, seashell, rai stones and cows.

THE MONEY MODEL

From ancient to current, every monetary system contains three elements.

- **Currency:** It is the medium of money.
- **Network:** Money without people is useless. Therefore, at least a bunch of people should transact with it.
- **Storage:** Money needs secure storage. Storage and security go hand in hand.

Figure 2.1 Centralized Money Model

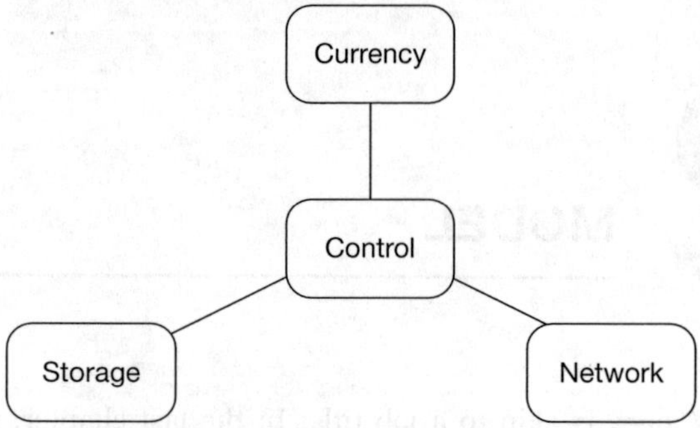

Here, you must understand the meaning of a crucial term, 'centralization', which means that *the power to control the system lies with few*. To identify centralization of money, you should ask three questions:

1. Who creates the money?
2. Who has the authority over which transactions are valid?
3. Who manages the platform for storing and exchanging money?

If your answers to the above questions point towards specific entities, then TMM is centralized. In Figure 2.1, you can see a centralized money model (CMM). The story of cryptocurrencies is the story of establishing a decentralized money model (DMM).

Currency

Currencies are monetary mediums which can become candidates of money. All candidates fall under one of the two groups.

1. Token: These include various forms of physical currency such as banknotes and coins. Tokens are verified for authenticity at the time of payment and don't require you to disclose personally identifying information while spending. For example, after having dinner in a restaurant, you hand over $100 to the owner. The only thing they need to do is to verify whether the $100 is authentic or fake. They are not bothered about who you are, what your profession is, etc.

2. Ledger: It is a record of ownership and obligations. It can be physical or digital. It requires you to prove your ownership by establishing your identity. For example, a bank deposit account is a kind of ledger money. It exists only in the ledger of the bank. When you receive your monthly salary in your bank account, your company's bank account balance is reduced, increasing your account. When you pay EMIs, your account balance is reduced, and bank's account balance is increased. Until recently, banks were using physical registers made from paper. However, after the advent of computers, almost all the banks went digital. Here are two crucial points that distinguish ledger money from token money.

- While token money requires you to *identify the currency* as counterfeit or genuine, ledger money needs you to *identify the account owner* as fake or real. Therefore, private information is provided while opening a bank account.
- When you spend from your bank balance, you don't care which specific amount you spend. For example, your bank balance consists of $50,000 received for salary, $5,000 rental income and $3,000 sales proceeds from your old car. Your total account balance is $58,000. Suppose you want to transfer $10,000 to your dad; you don't select from which income you will move this $10,000. Each unit of your bank account balance is fungible with other units.

Concept note: The issuance of token money is centralized, as only government authorized institutions like central banks can issue currencies. But its storage and transactions are decentralized. On the contrary, all aspects of ledger money, from issuance to storage to transactions, are centralized with the banks and financial institutions.

'A third kind of money' was invented just 10 years ago. This money is neither a digital token nor a digital ledger. It is both similar and different from token and ledger money.

Network

Money works because people use it for storing, transferring and measuring value. A country is the most extensive network of people who use the same currency. But the management and control lie with a small network of banks and financial institutions. Every transaction in ledger money needs to pass through banks' ledgers and be approved by banking authorities, which provides these financial intermediaries significant power over money. The network within CMM is centralized because a tiny network of institutions controls the monetary transactions of billions of people.

Concept note: Cryptocurrencies are managed by a decentralized network called a 'peer-to-peer network'. The ledgers maintained by the network are called 'decentralized ledger'.

Storage

Every 'thing' in the world occupies physical space. Even digital things—images, documents and videos—are stored in the physical area available within a computer. This is why you check how much data it can hold while buying a mobile. Money is valuable because it carries value. It is natural for us to store valuable things securely. While a small amount of token money, such as banknotes and coins, is stored with the public, a substantial portion of the money is stored in the databases of banks and financial institutions. Money stored with people is distributed and decentralized, whereas the amount stored with the banks is clustered and centralized. Two of the main reasons people store a large amount of cash with banks are security and ease of payment. Once the money is deposited with the banks, it is converted into ledger money or a deposit account. It is an asset for you but a liability for the bank. Since most bank ledgers are now digitally stored, bank deposits are a form of centralized digital money.

Concept note: As we will see, cryptocurrencies are stored in a distributed and decentralized ledger called the blockchain. These ledgers are highly secured and protected by heavy cryptography.

The upcoming chapters will discuss and elaborate further on the three elements of TMM.

- Evolution of *currency* in Chapter 3
- Drawbacks of *centralized currency, network* and *storage* in Chapter 4
- Quest for *DMM* in Chapter 5
- The problem that prevents digital things from working as a *currency* in Chapter 6
- How cryptocurrencies have emerged as a *DMM* in Chapter 7
- *The process of decentralizing the CMM* in Chapters 8 and 9.

3 EVOLUTION

Money is a recent innovation in human history (10,000 BCE).[1] Before the invention of money, there were two kinds of systems:

1. Gifts and credits
2. Barter

GIFTS AND CREDITS: A SYSTEM OF LEDGER MONEY

Simple societies had a currency called promise.[2] If I borrow something from you, I promise to pay you back. As societies became more and more complicated, it was difficult to remember the promises made by us or the promises made to us. There is strong historical evidence that the need to do accounting or maintain a ledger of things we own and owe was a significant reason behind the invention of writing and money.[3] Around 3,000 BC, Mesopotamians used clay tablets to record daily transactions like price they paid

1 G. Thomas Friedlob and Franklin J. Plewa, Jr., *Understanding Balance Sheets* (New York: John Wiley & Sons, 1996), 1.
2 Yves Smith, 'What Is Debt? An Interview with Economic Anthropologist David Graeber', Naked Capitalism, 26 August 2011, https://www.nakedcapitalism.com/2011/08/what-is-debt-%E2%80%93-an-interview-with-economic-anthropologist-david-graeber.html
3 Keith Robson, 'Accounting Numbers as "Inscription": Action at a Distance and the Development of Accounting', *Accounting, Organizations and Society* 17, no. 7 (1992): 685–708.

for a bushel of wheat. Yap islanders had a ledger system to track ownership and money transfer.

Entries in the ledger measured the value of something tangible owed and owned. For example, while a flock of sheep could be a liability in my ledger as I was obliged to return it to you in the future, it was an asset in your ledger. However, it was extremely difficult to check the reliability of ledgers until the Italian mathematician Luca Pacioli published a book on double-entry bookkeeping. He created an elegant ledger system which tracked and tallied the source of funds (credits) and uses of funds (debits) in real time. It helped merchants match each use of fund with a corresponding source of fund involved in a transaction. The accuracy of this system led to the formulation of joint-stock companies and large-scale banking systems. By the time we reached the 20th and 21st centuries, ledger money had become the most widely used money. The problem with ledger money is that of centralization. Almost all kinds of ledger money systems are CMMs, except a few cases like Yap islanders.

BARTER: A SYSTEM OF TOKEN MONEY

Barter payment: A thing accepted as a payment in a *particular transaction*

If I want something you have and you want something I have, then we can exchange our goods. It can work well for small tribes which trade necessities for a living.

Limitations

It is challenging to have a *double coincidence of wants*. For example, I want to buy your horse, and you want 10 goats in return. If I don't have goats or I don't like to exchange them, we can't do barter because our wants don't match. As the society grew, different kinds of occupations evolved. These occupations or professions produced specialized goods and services which needed to be exchanged with many more people. It was not possible to do barter. This might have forced us to accept a *common valuable commodity* as a medium of exchange.[4]

EVOLUTION OF TOKEN MONEY

Commodity Money: Money Is a Valuable Thing

Commodity money: A thing accepted as payment in a *variety of transactions*

The tokenized *monetary media* was born as a solution to the problem of double co-incidence of wants. At various points of history, livestock, grain, seashells, gold and other precious metals, even cigarettes, were used as money. These commodities helped us to acquire additional goods which other people had.

Limitations

- It isn't easy to carry commodity money. Even farmers of Mesopotamia didn't do it in 3,000 BCE. They would deposit grain in a temple which recorded the deposit on clay tablets and gave them a receipt in the form of a clay token. They used this receipt to pay fees and settle debts.[5] This receipt is called representative money.
- Since the commodity being used has its value, its intrinsic value could exceed its monetary value.

Representative Money: Money Represents a Valuable Thing

Representative money: A certificate, note or receipt representing valuable goods

4 Samuel Noah Kramer, *History Begins at Sumer* (Philadelphia: University of Pennsylvania Press, 1988), 52–55.
5 Denise Schmandt-Besserat, 'Tokens: Their Significance for the Origin of Counting and Writing', n.d., https://sites.utexas.edu/dsb/tokens/tokens/

Instead of carrying and making payments with grain bags, you can issue a certificate that states 'I owe you x number of grain bags' and put your signature. Every monetary medium except commodity money is 'I owe you money'. It is a liability for the issuer, which they promise to repay in the future. Certificates made money portable but, at the same time, added a layer of trust. People don't need to trust grain's value, but they must trust your certificates. Trust comes with a cost. It has the risk of counter-party default. Until people trust your credentials, they won't bother to visit you unless they need grain. But even if there is the slightest shadow of doubt or rumour about your ability to repay, everyone will come knocking at your door simultaneously. You better have those grain bags in your warehouse (we will see how it can result in banks going bankrupt in the next chapter).

As cities grew and commerce expanded, people needed to trust strangers. It was challenging to establish trust among strangers as you can't verify their credentials. This gave birth to a new entity, a trusted third party, who collected commodities from people and issued certificates. For the farmers of Mesopotamia, this was the temple; for modern societies, it is the central and commercial banks. These certificates were accepted by strangers, as a reliable third party promised to repay goods in exchange. Paper notes backed by the gold reserves were the last major form of commodity-backed representative money (usually called gold certificates). Almost all the countries worldwide followed the gold standard until the 1970s until Richard Nixon scrapped it in the USA.

Limitations

- Its value relied on the promise of a central authority, and issuance was centralized. Counter-party risk was eliminated but replaced with third-party risk.
- Governments could print money only to the extent of gold reserves available. Inflexibility to create new currencies made

it difficult for governments to tackle economic difficulties. In periods of recession, people hoarded gold by redeeming dollars, which depleted gold reserves and decreased the capacity to print money, making economic recovery difficult.

Fiat Money: Money Represents Trust in Government and the Economy

Fiat means 'let it be done'. It's the name for government currencies we are using today. It is not linked to anything valuable and not a promise to pay anything particular. It is a liability of central and commercial banks to redeem value. This is why banks replace truncated notes with new notes. A torn note doesn't extinguish the liability of banks. What differentiates fiat from gold certificates is the convertibility to commodity. While you could have exchanged a gold certificate for gold, you could only get new fiat currency in exchange for fiat currencies. Fiat is the most widely accepted form of money because governments have made it *legal tender*. It means that you must pay your taxes and settle your debts using fiat currencies. Fiat money comes in two forms: token and ledger.

Token Fiat Money: Notes and Coins Issued by Central Banks

These are the physical currencies issued by central banks. Central banks are nationalized banks specifically authorized by law to issue currency. Central banks issue almost all the currencies which are in circulation nowadays. However, private currencies were issued during the 17th and 18th centuries. There were around 8,000 currencies in the USA by the 1960s.[6] Holding these currencies was risky because they would become worthless if such an organization went bankrupt or decided to shut down. These organizations were

6 Private currency, https://en.wikipedia.org/wiki/Private_currency

called ‘wildcat banks’ because of their highly unreliable nature. Similar systems existed in Australia until 1910. There are three commercial banks in Hong Kong and seven commercial banks in the UK which issue their currencies even today.[7]

Concept note: Cryptocurrencies are considered private currencies because governments do not back them. We will see how cryptocurrencies are not private in the sense of private currencies of the 17th–18th centuries.

Ledger Fiat Money

These are the amounts recorded in banks’ ledgers. A substantial portion of government money exists only in ledgers, not as banknotes or coins. Ledger fiat money differs from its ancestors concerning the redeemability of liability. Until the gold standard, an entry in the bank’s ledger represented an obligation to pay something tangible, like gold, whereas under the fiat money system, banks are not liable to redeem anything for the amounts sitting in their ledgers.

7 International Bank Note Society, ‘Hong Kong’s 1,000 (HSBC) Dollar Note’, n.d., https://www.theibns.org/joomla/index.php?option=com_content&view=article&id=232&catid=13&Itemid=51;
The Association of Commercial Banknote Issuers, ‘Scottish and Northern Ireland Banknotes Fact Sheet’, n.d., https://web.archive.org/web/20180128040158/http://www.acbi.org.uk/media/sni_notes_factsheet_nov12_copy1.pdf

4 PROBLEMS

The whole financial system relies on a few central authorities such as the government, central bank, commercial banks and financial institutions. We didn't have any alternative but trust them with our money (until cryptocurrencies were invented). Following are the top 10 problems of CMM. The motivation behind creating cryptocurrencies was to solve these problems.

PROBLEM 1: IT IS NOT SCARCE

Fiat money is not scarce. Governments can print any amount they want. While it provides flexibility to tackle economic problems, it can lead to misuse of power. We are at the mercy of the government and central bank to maintain the value of these currencies. Printing more money doesn't necessarily create value. The value lies in useful goods and services, not in paper notes. If a country produces more money than its goods' value, the same goods will cost more. Therefore, careless printing of money can lead to situations like hyperinflation, where the value of money becomes almost worthless.

Case 1: The Reckless Printing of Money by the Zimbabwean Government

It created so much money that merchants used to weigh bundles of cash instead of counting them. A loaf of bread would have cost you

550 million Zimbabwean dollars. At the pick of its economic ruin, Zimbabwe created the highest denominated currency in history—a $100 trillion note (which you can buy on Amazon with a few bucks).[1]

Case 2: Venezuelan Bolivar

A similar thing happened in Venezuela over the last decade because of its political instability. Two Venezuelan bolivars were equivalent to one US dollar in 2009. In October 2021, you needed 4.18 million bolivars to buy 1 US dollar. Its inflation is one of the worst in history. Over 6 million Venezuelans, 20 per cent of the total population, were forced to leave the country.[2]

PROBLEM 2: IT DOESN'T WORK DESPITE BEING LEGAL TENDER

Governments worldwide have made fiat currencies legal tender. Its value is created by legislative force as you must pay your taxes and settle your debts using these currencies. Despite that, it may not work.

Case 3: 25 Paise

Let me give you an example from India. There was a rumour that 25 paise and 50 paise coins were no longer valid. No street vendor, shopkeeper or bus conductor would accept it. At last, the central bank of India came forward and clarified that these currencies were still valid. Despite this clarification, acceptance of these coins remained low. Slowly, these currencies were out of circulation.[3]

1 Elliot McLaughlin, 'Harare Woman; If You Talk Too Much ... They Hunt You Down', CNNOnline, 25 June 2008, http://edition.cnn.com/2008/WORLD/africa/06/25/zimbabwe.voices/index.html?iref=allsearch

2 Kathryn Reid, 'Forced to Flee: Top Countries Refugees Are Coming from', 18 June 2021, https://www.worldvision.org/refugees-news-stories/forced-to-flee-top-countries-refugees-coming-from

3 RBI, 'Coins of All Denominations Are Legal Tender – RBI', 16 September 2004, https://www.rbi.org.in/commonperson/English/Scripts/PressReleases.aspx?Id=222#:~:text=

Case 4: Crumbled Notes

This is another common situation in India. No one will accept a torn banknote, even though the central bank had made it clear that you should accept it if its serial number is intact. But since no one would accept it, no one accepts it.

PROBLEM 3: GOVERNMENTS CAN CENSOR IT

Fiat currencies are entirely under government control. It can censor, stop or modify the rules of the money game.

Case 5: Won

The North Korean government issued a new currency in 2009 to replace its old money. A new won became equivalent to 100 old wons. No one is harmed if old currencies can be swapped with new currencies. The Government of India had discontinued 500- and 1,000-rupee notes in 2016. Still, it provided enough time to exchange the old rupee notes for new ones. Brazil did a similar thing in 1994 when it discontinued old cruzeiro reals. Brazilians were allowed to convert 2,750 cruzeiro reals for one real (new currency). But North Korea did something peculiar. It allowed only a limited amount of old cash to be converted to the new currency.

Further, it had given only 24 hours to swap the old money. This was a move to curb black market traders, but it had an insidious impact on ordinary citizens. They lost most of their savings in a single day.[4]

Coins%20of%20All%20Denominations%20are%20Legal%20Tender%20%E2%80%93%20RBI&text=do%20not%20readily%20accept%2025,not%20accepted%20by%20bank%20branches

4 Choe Sang-Hun, 'North Korea Revalues Its Currency', *The New York Times*, 2 December 2009.

PROBLEM 4: CASH DOESN'T WORK AT DISTANCE

There were only two modes of payment before the invention of cryptocurrencies.

Cash payments: Transfer of value through physical currencies
Intermediated payments: Transfer of value through intermediaries

Cash Payments

Cash transactions are done peer to peer; there is no intermediary between you and the seller. Payments are settled instantly, and no third party can intervene to stop them. Although cash transactions have many benefits, they suffer from a significant drawback. That is, cash doesn't work in the distance.

- You cannot pay in cash if the sender and receiver are not in the exact location.
- You cannot pay in cash if the sender and receiver are not present simultaneously.

As you can see, it is not possible to transfer value over time and distance with cash payments. This problem is solved by involving a trusted middleman. For example, you have just received your salary and want to send some cash to your mom, who lives in another city. You can take the help of Bob, a family friend, who is traveling to your mom's city. Bob can deliver the cash to your mom. Bob is a trusted middleman in this cash transfer. However, it is not always possible to find a person like Bob who can be trusted. Even if you find a trustworthy person, they may not want to carry out the transaction. Because of these shortcomings, a standardized, trusted and regulated intermediary system of banks and financial institutions emerged.

Intermediated Payments

Intermediated payments require a trusted third party. Banks and financial institutions work as trusted intermediaries in most monetary transactions that happen over a distance. The need for carrying cash to make payments is also eliminated as it is deposited with banks. With the advent of the digital age, almost all intermediated payments are now happening online.

PROBLEM 5: CARELESS CREATION OF MONEY BY PRIVATE BANKS

Here comes the mind-bending part of fiat money. Commercial banks create more money than you can imagine, generating it through loans. You must be thinking that we don't see any currency with a private bank logo or name. That is true. Your country's central bank issues the currencies you are holding. But these currencies are only 10–15 per cent of the total money supply. The rest of the money supply is just in the banks' ledgers.

Let me explain:

- Central banks create money and lend it to commercial banks (through open market operations).
- Commercial banks hold a fraction of that money and lend the rest as loans to other banks. This is called a fractional banking system.
- Other banks follow the same process, keeping a fraction of the money with them and lending the rest as loans to people.

Note: The fraction of money held by banks is called reserves, and its percentage varies from country to country.

Example: How fractional banking creates money from credit

- I have $100,000 cash. You have $0.
- I went to a bank and deposited $100,000. I can withdraw this money anytime and write cheques on it.

- The same bank kept $10,000 as a reserve and loans you $90,000 (assuming 10% is the reserve requirement).

What has just happened?

- I have $100,000 as a bank deposit which I can spend.
- You have $90,000 cash which you can spend.

$90,000 new money is created out of $100,000 just by credit.

Let's extend the example:

- You deposited $90,000 in another bank.
- Bank kept $9,000 in reserve and lent $81,000 to Bob.

As a result:

- I have $100,000 as a bank deposit which I can spend.
- You have $90,000 as a bank deposit which you can spend.
- Bob has $81,000 cash which he can spend.

$81,000 new money is created out of your $90,000 deposit. Theoretically, suppose everyone deposits their money with banks, and banks lend 90 per cent every time. In that case, new money generated in the economy will be the initial cash × 1/reserve requirement. I had initial cash of $100,000 and reserve requirement was 10 per cent; hence, total money that can be created is $100,000/0.10 = $10,00,000. $900,000 new money can be created out of $100,000 just by bank lending. As you can see, 'loans create money.' This $900,000 new money exists only in banks' records. Therefore, broad money consists of physical currencies plus one or more types of bank deposits.

Now imagine that one prominent bank goes broke due to some financial mismanagement. It sparks a rumour that a recession like 2008 is on the verge. The word spreads like fire. The media covers it day and night. Slowly people start to panic: What if our banks also go broke? You and I both rush to our banks to collect our deposits. I ask my bank to pay me back $100,000; my bank asks you to pay back $90,000; you ask your bank to pay back $90,000; your bank asks Bob to pay back $81,000. But unfortunately, Bob has lost all his money in a casino. Now, your bank can pay you only $9,000; since it couldn't pay back customer deposits, it declared insolvency. You lost $81,000 and could only return $9,000 to my bank. My bank paid me $19,000 and went insolvent. I lost $81,000. Total money lost = $81,000 × 3 (Bob, you and me) = $243,000.

A situation like this is called a bank run; when customers fear that the bank is in trouble, they flood to withdraw their deposits. Bob's gambling loss is passed on to you and me without our mistake. We trust banks for safekeeping our money, but they can misuse it by lending without proper credit assessment.

Case 6: A Recession

The 2008 crisis was caused by subprime loans, which had a lower chance of repayment. Still, banks extended loans to people knowing that they couldn't pay them back and sold derivatives backed by these loans to investors to make a profit. The sixth-most prominent financial institution of the USA, Washington Mutual, shut down on 25 September 2008, as customers had withdrawn around $16.7 billion, resulting in a shortfall of cash reserves.[5]

PROBLEM 6: CORRUPTION

Corruption in banks is well known. There have been many scams where bank personnel colluded with corrupt business people to render credits beyond allowed limits. Of course, when these people

5 Jim Zarroli, 'Washington Mutual Collapses', All Things Considered. National Public Radio, 26 September 2008, https://www.npr.org/templates/story/story.php?storyId=95105112&msclkid=c98021f6d09411eca763614a3ad60aac; Kimberly Amadeo, 'The Causes of the Subprime Mortgage Crisis', 29 January 2022, https://www.thebalance.com/what-caused-the-subprime-mortgage-crisis-3305696

don't pay back, it is the hard-earned money of the public that is lost. There have been cases of money laundering too. Recently, five major banks—Deutsche Bank, HSBC, JPMorgan, Bank of New York Mellon and Standard Chartered—were exposed by Financial Crimes Enforcement Network (FinCEN) for laundering $2 trillion.[6]

PROBLEM 7: DIGITAL MONEY IS PRONE TO A SINGLE POINT OF FAILURE

Tools for carrying out payments have evolved from cheques to online banking, credit cards, debit cards, PayPal, Google Pay, Apple Pay, etc. The role of trusted third parties has become indispensable for online payments as we must rely solely on their platforms. From buying a slipper on Amazon to booking movie tickets, sending money to family and paying to vendors, all monetary transactions on the Internet must pass through these central actors' ledgers. A lot of money now exists digitally, controlled and managed by trusted third parties. These ledgers are centralized databases. The problem with centralized databases is that they are vulnerable as a single point of failure. Since a vast amount of money is stored in one place, they are prone to cyberattacks, system failure, natural disasters, etc. Several banks have lost billions of dollars in the last few decades due to these reasons.

PROBLEM 8: DIGITAL MONEY CREATES PRIVACY CONCERNS

Banks and credit card companies collect sensitive private information in the form of KYC. While we trust banks to not deliberately divulge or sell our information, the risk of hacking and online fraud cannot be ignored. Many people are getting scammed in various ways because

6 WION, 'FinCEN Documents Show How Global Banks Moved Illicit Funds despite Red Flags, 21 September 2020, https://www.wionews.com/business-economy/fincen-documents-show-how-global-banks-moved-illicit-funds-despite-red-flags-329028

their mobile numbers, email addresses and other personal data are leaked. You might have received bogus weblinks of banks and network service providers followed by a frantic call from spammers to update KYC information. Many people fall prey to this and share their bank account detail with one-time passwords and lose substantial amounts.

Case 7: Equifax Data Breach

Massive data breach occurred at Equifax between May and July 2017 when private records of 147 million Americans along with 15 million British citizens and about 19,000 Canadian citizens were compromised. It is one of the largest cybercrimes related to identity theft.[7]

Case 8: JP Morgan Hack

Hackers stole the private information of 76 million JPMorgan customers in 2014.[8]

Case 9: Capital One Incident

Sensitive information of 100 million customers of Capital One was compromised in 2019.[9]

PROBLEM 9: HIGH TRANSACTION COST AND DELAY IN SETTLEMENT

Intermediaries pocket a significant portion of all the monetary transactions in transfer charges, maintenance charges, account opening fees and tax on these fees. Settlement takes time due to

7 Federal Trade Commission, 'Equifax Data Breach Settlement', February 2022, https://www.ftc.gov/enforcement/cases-proceedings/refunds/equifax-data-breach-settlement
8 Dominic Rushe, 'JP Morgan Chase Reveals Massive Data Breach Affecting 76m Households', The Guardian, 3 October 2014, https://www.theguardian.com/business/2014/oct/02/jp-morgan-76m-households-affected-data-breach
9 Rob McLean, 'A Hacker Gained Access to 100 Million Capital One Credit Card Applications and Accounts', 30 July 2019, https://edition.cnn.com/2019/07/29/business/capital-one-data-breach/index.html

involvement of several intermediaries. There are three parties in the middle of buyer and merchant in a credit card transaction: the issuer, the acquirer and the switch. The issuer is the customer's bank, the acquirer is the merchant's bank and the switch is a visa company connecting both the banks. If you buy a mobile for $100 using a credit card, your merchant will receive around $97.76 only. Rest $2.24 will be shared among the issuer, acquirer and switch. Since everyone has to approve the transaction from their end, it will take two–three days for the merchant to receive money. Therefore, you may have seen shopkeepers refusing to accept credit cards, or they will demand you to pay 2 per cent more.

If you make an international payment through PayPal, it will cost you around 3 per cent. It will cost you the same if you are accepting payment. PayPal earns from both of the parties. You must bear a varied rate of fees for using similar intermediaries such as Western Union, Xoom and MoneyGram. Average bank transfers take around three days to settle. At the same time, cross-border transactions involve a substantial amount of time and cost because the list of intermediaries is enormous. Payments are sent through a centralized Society for Worldwide Interbank Financial Telecommunications (SWIFT) system, which involves intermediaries such as banks and custodians, brokers and dealers, insurance companies, investment managers, pension funds, transfer agents, user groups, International Central Securities Depository (ICSDs) and central securities depository (CSDs), Electronic Trade Confirmation (ETC) providers, infrastructures and corporates and stock exchanges. Each intermediary adds to the cost and acts as a single point of failure.

PROBLEM 9: REVERSIBLE PAYMENTS

In the case of cash-to-cash transactions, merchants need not worry about the payments getting reversed. However, in the case of digital payments, there is always a chance of payments getting reversed due to various reasons such as fraud and insufficient balance in the buyer's account. This may lead to disputes between transacting parties, which increases the transaction cost as intermediaries charge the mediation fee from both parties.

PROBLEM 10: UNBANKED PEOPLE

There are two billion people in the world who don't have access to intermediaries' services.[10] They neither have bank accounts nor do they own credit cards. Banks and financial institutions decide their own rules to provide access to their services. Poor people often don't fit their criteria.

10 Axuant, 'The World's Unbanked Population', 25 November 2020, https://www.acuant.com/blog/the-worlds-unbanked-population/

5 SEARCH

Owing to various problems of CMM, a group of computer scientists and cryptologists were trying to develop a digital version of cash from the 1980s. They envisioned a DMM, free from government control and censorship. Despite putting in enormous effort, they didn't see success until the invention of Bitcoin.

Here is the list of digital currencies that failed:

- DigiCash by David Chaum (1989)
- Mondex by National Westminster Bank (1993)
- CryberCash by Lynch, Melton, Crocker and Wilson (1994)
- E-gold by Gold & Silver Reserve (1996)
- Hashcash by Adam Back (1997)
- BitGold by Nick Szabo (1998)
- B-Money by Wei Dai (1998)
- Lucre by Ben Laurie (1999)

Despite the failure, let's discuss a few of them which laid the foundation for cryptocurrencies.

DAVID CHAUM'S DIGICASH

David Chaum, one of the pioneers of digital currencies, published his famous paper 'Blind Signatures of Untraceable Payments' in 1982.

He conceptualized a digital currency which could be transferred between individuals privately. His so-called 'blinding formula' was a method for making anonymous digital transactions. David founded a company called DigiCash in 1989. DigiCash was not P2P electronic cash. It still relied on the banks as trusted third parties for all the electronic transactions. It was able to secure partnerships with a few banks such as Deutsche Bank, Credit Suisse and Norske Bank but ultimately failed to convince other banks to adopt its technology. It went bankrupt in 1998. However, the technology for making anonymous transactions is used in cryptocurrencies.[1]

ADAM BACK'S HASHCASH

British cryptographer Adam Back published 'Hashcash' to the cypherpunks' mailing list in 1997, where he proposed a solution for email spam[2]:

- The sender must do some work to send a valid email.
- Because the work will take some computer processing time, spammers will be discouraged from sending junk mails.

The work done by the sender proves their intention to send a valid email. Hence, it is called 'proof of work' (POW). Although Hashcash was not originally intended to be used for monetary transactions, its 'POW' concept played a crucial role in developing cryptocurrencies. As we will see later, blockchains use POW to secure and validate cryptocurrency transactions. It helps to prevent double-spending.

1 David Chaum, 'Blind Signatures for Untraceable Payments', *Advances in Cryptology Proceedings of Crypto* 82, no. 3 (1983): 199–203; Julie Pitta, 'Requiem for a Bright Idea', *Forbes* (1 November 1999), https://www.forbes.com/forbes/1999/1101/6411390a.html?sh=780cd1a6715f

2 Hashcash.org, 'A Partial Hash Collision Based Postage Scheme', 28 March 1997, http://www.hashcash.org/papers/announce.tx

B-MONEY AND BITGOLD

Developer Wei Dai proposed B-Money in 1998. This distributed electronic cash system would have enabled anonymous transfer of digital cash. However, this project never took off.[3] Around the same period, Nick Szabo proposed BitGold. Nick intended to create a digital currency similar to gold, requiring no intermediary to transact.[4] BitGold, like B-Money, was ultimately unsuccessful, though both have inspired the creation of Bitcoin.

These currencies failed because they couldn't handle four problems:

1. **Centralization:** Some of these currencies relied on intermediaries like banks and financial institutions.
2. **Double-spending:** They couldn't solve the problem of double-spending without involving trusted middlemen.
3. **Consensus:** Once you remove central bookkeepers, ledgers must be validated by the group of users. However, deciding whose ledger is valid and whose invalid requires a consensus from all the users. A currency system usually caters to millions of people, and finding a way to establish consensus among them was one of the most complex problems of computer science. All these currencies failed to solve the 'problem of decentralized consensus'.
4. **Lack of use:** There was no community or network of users backing them. Merchant adoption was low.

3 http://www.weidai.com/

4 Phillio Moscov, 'What Is Bit Gold? The Brainchild of Blockchain Pioneer Nick Szabo', 22 May 2018, https://coincentral.com/what-is-bit-gold-the-brainchild-of-blockchain-pioneer-nick-szabo/

6 COPY–PASTE

One of the reasons we maintain the ledger money with banks and other intermediaries is that they help us to ensure two things: No one spends the same money twice and no one spends the money they don't have.

NO BANKING SYSTEM!

Suppose Murphy went shopping and landed at Bob's shop. After bargaining for half an hour, he finally brought a new laptop by handing Bob a $100 banknote. We are sure that he didn't possess that same banknote at the end of this transaction anymore. There is no issue in cash-to-cash exchange. However, things become messy if Murphy wants to send $100 online. (Remember that there is no banking system).

Assume that Murphy took a photo of $100. Now the paper note is converted to an electronic note. Let's call this $100 an e-note. There is a problem: Digital things are not scarce. We can copy them limitlessly, making them unsuitable as currency. So Murphy can create multiple copies of the e-note.

Murphy is cunning. He sent the e-note to Bob and kept one copy in his smartphone. Then he continued shopping and brought a pair of shoes by spending the copy. This is called the double-spending problem. He spent the same currency twice. If Murphy can do that, you, me and everyone can do that. This e-note will be worthless soon.

Let's take a small example to see how it would be worthless. Assume that there is only one laptop available on earth. It is priced at $100. The world's population consists of only three persons: you, me and the seller. Both you and I want to buy it. I will offer the seller a $100 e-note. You will offer $200. I will offer $1,000. You will offer $1 million. I will offer $1 billion. You may offer a trillion. The bidding will continue because we can copy the $100 digital note countless times. Money's value comes from its purchasing power. Creating more money than the value of products available for purchasing decreases its purchasing power. It is called *inflation*. An unlimited supply of money will create *hyperinflation* and make it worthless.

E-note lacks two essential properties: currency scarcity and unforgeability. Everything digital lacks these properties. To solve the double-spending problem, we must ask Murphy to *delete* the copy from his device once he sends the e-note to Bob. What if he keeps a copy even after our request? *We can't trust him.* You will see that the *problem of trust* sits at the core of conventional currencies.

ALTERNATIVE SOLUTION?

Since digital tokens are infinitely copiable, why don't we shift from token money system to ledger money system? Let us see if this works. What if we create a website which will maintain a ledger for how much digital money everyone has and continuously update for e-note transfers? Below you can see both Bob and Murphy's ledger accounts on the website. Murphy's account balance is 0 after he transfers the $100 e-note.

The scenario will be different if Murphy tries to purchase shoes by transferring the copy in the future. The seller will first check

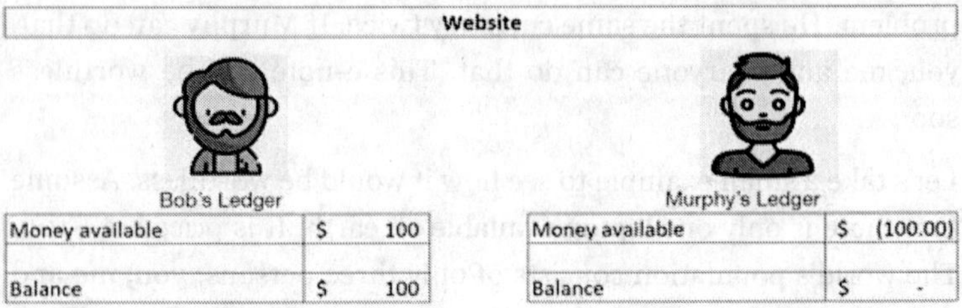

Murphy's ledger on the website and see whether he has $100 in his ledger. He will reject the transaction, as he can see Murphy's account balance is 0. It looks like the problem is solved. But why didn't we have such websites in reality?

There are many reasons:

- A centralized server will host the website. That server can be hacked, destroyed or censored by the government. (Single point of failure)
- Who will maintain the website? The person or organization that will host the website can manipulate the ledger balances. They would have the power to approve or deny access to the website. They can change the design and the platform's rules. How can we trust this central actor? (Problem of centralized authority)
- There will be no privacy, as everyone's ledger will be public. I will know Bob's balance and where he gets his money. You will know my balance and transactions. Everyone will know everyone's. This will put lives in danger. (No privacy)
- Governments can easily crack down on such projects as they can locate the servers. (Censorship)

Solving the double-spending problem without intermediaries was a major obstacle in the way of achieving a digital DMM. However, no one could solve it until the birth of Bitcoin.

7 CRYPTOCURRENCIES

The monetary system became centralized as we moved from commodity to trust-based fiat money. An indispensable central authority was required to create, store and manage money to prevent the problem of double-spending. The concentration of trust and power with few individuals and organizations created the hazard of a reckless, corrupt and fragile monetary system. These hazards were culminated in a worldwide recession in 2008 because of the irresponsible financial system of the USA. In the same year, someone had invented an alternative monetary system. The idea of a digital currency managed by people and not by governments was so unrealistic that everyone, from the public, media and so-called intellectuals to computer geeks, took it as a joke. Anyone with a laptop could mine (create) many of these currencies for the first two years. Very few had realized the importance of this event. It was the beginning of a revolution.

INVENTION OF BITCOIN

Bitcoin was invented by a mysterious person or a group called Satoshi Nakamoto in October 2008. It is the world's first digital candidate for scarce money and the first asset known to humanity whose supply and issuance schedule are known entirely in advance. Its scarcity is not enforced by any intermediary but the Bitcoin software itself. The identity of its inventor is still unknown. Over the last decade, his status has risen to a mythical God-like figure who had good intentions, had the genius to solve the enormously complex double-spending problem and applied his skills to produce an alternative to fiat money without taking credit for it. His anonymity went on to prove that a leaderless global monetary system is possible. The *core motivations* behind Bitcoin can be traced to the innumerable problems that emerged from CMM (refer to Figure 2.1). As evident from his writings, Satoshi Nakamoto tried to solve these problems through Bitcoin.

PROBLEM 1: CENTRALIZED MONEY

While launching the prototype of Bitcoin in a crypto forum, Satoshi Nakamoto expressed his concern about centralized money: 'The root problem with conventional currency is all the trust that's required to make it work. The central bank must be trusted not to debase the currency, but the history of fiat currencies is full of breaches of that trust.'[1]

PROBLEM 2: CENTRALIZED NETWORK

In the 2008 Bitcoin white paper, Satoshi Nakamoto stated the problem of centralized networks: 'Commerce on the Internet has come to rely almost exclusively on financial institutions serving as trusted third parties to process electronic payments. While the system works well enough for most transactions, it still suffers from the inherent weaknesses of the trust-based model.'[2]

1 Satoshi Nakamoto Institute, 'Bitcoin Open Source Implementation of P2P Currency', 2 November 2009, https://satoshi.nakamotoinstitute.org/posts/p2pfoundation/1/#selection-9.0-15.23

2 Satoshi Nakamoto, 'Bitcoin: A Peer-to-Peer Electronic Cash System', n.d., https://bitcoin.org/bitcoin.pdf

PROBLEM 3: CENTRALIZED STORAGE AND SAFETY

He was worried about the privacy and security of bank ledgers. While launching the Bitcoin prototype in 2009, he wrote: 'We have to trust banks with our privacy, trust them not to let identity thieves drain our accounts.'[3]

Above three problems boil down to one problem: 'control'. The monopoly over creating and managing money was in the hand of a few. Bitcoin aimed to shift it to the hands of the public.

CRYPTOCURRENCY: A DMM!

At the time of writing this book, around 9,000 cryptocurrencies existed worldwide. All of them were developed after bitcoin by imitating, improving and altering the rules of Bitcoin. With the following lines, Satoshi introduced Bitcoin as a decentralized monetary system: 'I've developed a new open-source P2P e-cash system called Bitcoin. It's completely decentralized, with no central server or trusted parties, because everything is based on crypto proof instead of trust.'[4]

Bitcoin uses software and hardware to create a decentralized currency system.

Software: This is the Bitcoin client software used for creating, storing and transferring currency among the network of users. Different cryptocurrencies have different client software.

Hardware: Every user in the network needs a device to run the cryptocurrency software, a mobile or a PC, or some mining device. These devices or computers that runs the cryptocurrency software are called 'nodes'.

3 Satoshi Nakamoto Institute, 'Bitcoin Open Source Implementation of P2P Currency'.
4 Ibid.

Figure 7.1 Decentralized Money Model

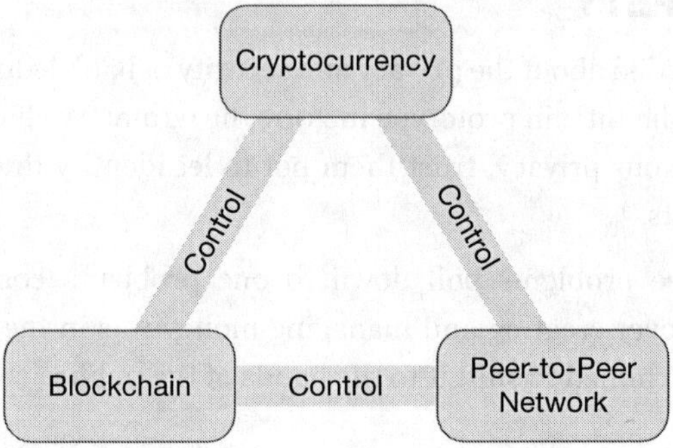

THE CRYPTOCURRENCY SOLUTION

Cryptocurrencies have taken the financial world by storm over the last decade. They have eliminated the monopoly of banks and financial institution over money and decentralized the elements of TMM (Figure 7.1).

Solution 1: Decentralizing the Creation of Money

In the words of Satoshi, cryptocurrencies are a 'purely peer-to-peer version of electronic cash that allows online payments to be sent directly from one party to another without going through a financial institution'. It is a decentralized form of electronic *cash,* created, stored and transacted on blockchain. Governments and central banks have no role in its issuance. It can be transferred between individuals without involving a bank or intermediary. The rules for creating currencies are coded in the cryptocurrency software.

Solution 2: Decentralizing the Network

Anyone can download the open-source software and connect with others to send and receive cryptos. Since no single party is in charge and no permission is needed to join, anyone can participate from anywhere globally, irrespective of their nationality, race, gender, etc. It is called a P2P network, as every computer in the network has equal rights. From creation to storage to spending, the management and control of cryptocurrencies are shifted to the P2P network. To prevent its users' private information from being misused, no one is required to disclose any personally identifying information. Everyone in the network is pseudonymous. Cryptocurrency transactions happen between public key to public key without ever needing to reveal the person's real-world identity.

Solution 3: Decentralizing Storage and Safety

Cryptocurrencies are stored in a decentralized and distributed ledger called the blockchain. Satoshi never used the word 'blockchain' in any of his writings. The white paper calls the underlying mechanism of Bitcoin a 'timestamp' server. The Bitcoin community used the term 'blockchain' after two years of its creation. It has been hailed as the most significant innovation since the Internet. Its application can be seen way beyond cryptocurrencies, ranging from supply chain management, secure healthcare records, public property registers, voting, triple-entry accounting, decentralized finance, the Internet of things, etc. While we will have a comprehensive discussion of blockchain later, let me give you a quick introduction.

Blockchain is an *electronic ledger* or database. It records the history of transactions in a chronological order. It is also a *distributed ledger,* as it is not stored in any central server. A copy of the database is distributed and stored in all the network nodes. Even if some nodes fail, the database is still updated and maintained by other nodes. This eliminates the risk of a single point of failure. Power to update the database is not available with any single user or group of users, making it a *decentralized ledger*. All or most of the users *must reach a consensus* before anything is added. It is almost impossible to hack or tamper with, as it is protected by military-grade cryptography. This is why it is called an *immutable ledger*. Transactions, once recorded, cannot be modified, which makes it an *append-only database.*

People often confuse cryptocurrency with blockchain. For example, the public misconstrues that Bitcoin and blockchain are the same things. Therefore, it is essential to distinguish between the two. Blockchain is a database that enables the creation and spending of cryptocurrencies. Cryptocurrencies are created by recording a transaction in the blockchain, called a coinbase transaction. Similarly, an entry in the blockchain is required to spend them.

8 LET'S CREATE A CRYPTOCURRENCY

Let's understand the working of cryptocurrencies by creating and spending a simple crypto coin. This is a non-technical explanation of how cryptos work. It will help us understand how blockchain and P2P networks solve the double-spending problem without the help of intermediaries.

CREATING CRYPTOCURRENCIES

Anyone can create a digital currency *by simply signing a digital document* that they are creating new currencies. For example, *let me create a new cryptocurrency*. After thinking a lot of creative names, we will call this new cryptocurrency, 'E-Coin.' Here is what I have done; I signed a digital document stating the creation of E-Coin with coin IDs: coin 1, coin 2, coin 3, coin 4 and coin 5. Once I write down the statement in a digital document and sign it digitally, the coins are created. Since this system is created by me, all the cryptocurrencies created by me are valid. They can be useless or illegal in some countries but not invalid.

Digital document
I am creating five electronic coins: coin 1, coin 2, coin 3, coin 4, coin 5
Digitally signed by me

Concept note: Do you remember that what is money is decided by the rules set by a bunch of people? These rules are called protocols.

Anyone can automate the protocols by writing software, which will issue and manage currencies as per the coded rules. If a network of people agrees with the protocol, they will start using the software and its currency as money. The software will be an open source and not owned by anyone. Therefore, cryptocurrencies are called programmable money. This digital document is called a transaction, and the transaction for creating new currencies is called a coinbase transaction.

SPENDING CRYPTOCURRENCIES

One who owns the money has the right to spend it. The same rule applies to cryptocurrencies. Presently, I own five coins. If I want to transfer these to Alice, I need to create another document, stating 'I gave five coins—coin 1, coin 2, coin 3, coin 4 and coin 5—to Alice' and sign it. I will include the original coin creation document with it. Similarly, Alice can transfer coins 1 and 2 to Bob; she needs to sign a document and include *all the previous documents as proof.*

Digital document
Alice gave coin 1 and coin 2 to Bob
Digitally signed by Alice

⬆

Digital document
I gave coin 1, coin 2, coin 3, coin 4, coin 5 to Alice
Digitally signed by me

⬆

Digital document
I am creating five electronnic coins: coin 1, coin 2, coin 3, coin 4, coin 5
Digitally signed by me

Concept note: Whether you transfer a house, piece of land or any other asset, you usually include previous documents to prove the *chain of ownership*. The same logic applies to the transfer of E-coin.

As you will learn later, a cryptographic technique called 'hash' acts as an identifier of digital things. Hash makes our work simple. Instead of including all previous documents or transactions, we just include the hash of those transactions in the current transaction. Transactions which spend the previously created coins are called *spend transactions*.

You can see that coins are owned and transferred by a chain of digitally signed transactions. Therefore, Satoshi Nakamoto, in 2008, defined an electronic coin as a chain of digital signatures: 'We define an electronic coin as a chain of digital signatures.'

The Double-Spend Attack

We know that Alice has transferred coins 1 and 2 to Bob. Let's see what can go wrong.

- What if she transfers coins 1 and 2 to Jack *again* by creating a separate transaction?
- She doesn't own these two coins anymore. But still, she would be able to spend the money she doesn't own.

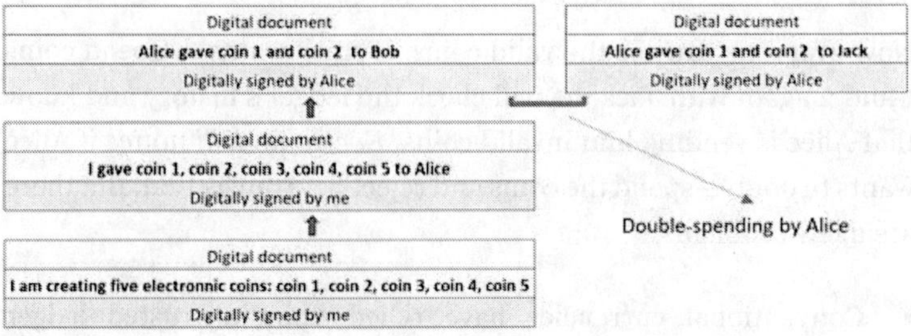

Alice will double-spend coins 1 and 2. Jack will think that these coins are valid because he is unaware of the transaction in the upper left (i.e., transfer of the same two currencies to Bob. Both Bob and

Jack have a valid claim on coins 1 and 2. Both are the owners of the same coins, which is not how money works. Traditionally, the double-spending problem in monetary transactions is solved by the centralized ledgers of banks and other intermediaries. But we don't use banks and other intermediaries in E-coin. Therefore, I, the currency creator, will publish a ledger which will contain the history of all coin transfers.

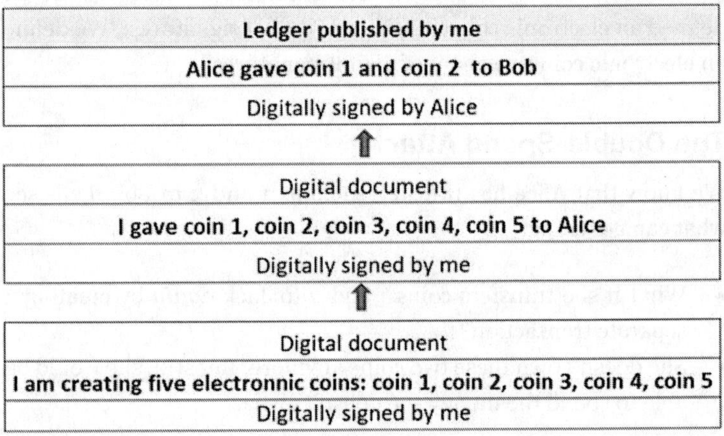

Now everyone can see the valid coins. If Alice wants to spend coins 1 and 2 again with Jack, he will check the ledger's history and know that Alice is sending him invalid coins. *Everyone will notice* if Alice wants to double-spend the coins and reject her transaction. But there are a few problems.

- Conventional currencies have relied upon a trusted ledger maintained by banks. Now, *you must trust my ledger* for the cryptocurrencies I have created.
- What if I get bored and decide to close this cryptocurrency endeavour?

- What if I change the rules that benefit my chosen ones and me? What if I get corrupted?

The whole system *relies on me*, a trusted central authority. I am doing the same job as banks and governments did. We aimed to solve the double-spending problem without involving any trusted third party. Therefore, Satoshi says in the Bitcoin white paper, 'The main benefits (of cryptocurrencies) are lost if a trusted third party is still required to prevent double-spending.' Hence, we must find a way to get rid of me. The solution should offer all the services I am offering but in a decentralized form, without relying on a single party.

SOLVING THE DOUBLE-SPENDING PROBLEM

To understand this, let me give the example of Yap islanders. In the first chapter, we discussed how large rai stones were used as currency by the people of Yap island. Those stones were huge, and moving them was trouble. Hence, whenever someone wanted to transfer the ownership of their rai stone, they just announced it to the whole town. Everyone in the town noted down the fact. In rare instances, stones were moved. While moving the stones, sometimes they would fall in the river and sink. However, the stone could still work as a currency because everyone assumed it still existed somewhere under the river.

For example, suppose I have transferred a rai stone to Jammie. Being a little eccentric, Jammie demanded the stone to be moved to his place. Unfortunately, on the way to Jammie's house, if fell into a river and got lost.

Let's analyse the case:

- Rai stone is a currency even if lost in the river. (This is one of the earliest instances of separation of currency as a concept from the currency as a valuable thing.) The stone, which was lost in the river, had value because everyone agreed to believe in its value.[1]

- When I announced the transfer of stone to the town, everyone noted down two things: One, the new owner is Jammie; two, the value of the stone. (This is an example of the distributed and decentralized ledger.) Here, the ledger exists only in people's memory but is distributed and available to everyone in the town. No single town person can claim something different about the facts that everyone else remembers. Hence, the power to change this shared database is not entrusted with any single trusted third party. We can call it a mental or oral blockchain.

Suppose Jammie wants to buy two elephants from Rudy, which costs a mid-sized rai stone. He will ask Rudy to come with him and announce to the whole town about his intention to buy two elephants. People will check their mental records and confirm:

- Jammie owns a rai stone which was transferred by the author
- Value of the stone
- Jammie has not transferred the ownership to anyone else before

In this way, the town people will ensure that Jammie has enough money to spend, and he is not paying the same money twice. Once they confirm it, Rudy is assured of the authenticity of Jammie's ownership and accepts the payment. People will again record two things: One, Rudy is the new owner; two, the value of the stone. In this way, the people of Yap island could solve the double-spending problem *without involving trusted third parties*. Instead of relying on a trusted bookkeeper, they made everyone a bookkeeper. We will apply a similar process to cryptocurrencies.

1 Gillilland, *The Stone Money of Yap*; Goldstein and Kestenbaum, 'The Island of Stone Money'.

SOLVING THE DOUBLE-SPENDING PROBLEM FOR CRYPTOCURRENCIES

Transaction: Alice wants to send coins 1 and 2 to Bob

- She will announce it to the P2P network. (It is called broadcasting the transaction. Her wallet software will do it with a click.)
- Every node in the P2P network will check their past records or blockchain for two things: one, whether she owns those two coins; two, whether she hasn't spent those coins already. If the check is positive, they will note down the new transaction in the blockchain. (Do you remember that an updated copy of the blockchain is available with every node in the P2P network?)
- If she tries to send coins 1 and 2 again to Jack, the P2P network will check if these coins are not yet spent. While scanning the blockchain, they will find that these coins are already sent to Bob. The transaction will be rejected.

If Bob wants to transfer these 2 coins in the future, the P2P network will follow the same process of checks and update the accounts for changes. In this way, 'we have avoided the dependency on me' for

	Blockchain
Transaction 3	**Alice gave coin 1 and coin 2 to Bob**
	Bob's Balance: coin 1, coin 2
	Alice's balance: coin 3, coin 4, coin 5
	Digitally signed by Alice
Transaction 2	**I gave coin 1, coin 2, coin 3, coin 4, coin 5 to Alice**
	Alice's balance: coin 1, coin 2, coin 3, coin 4, coin 5
	My balance: 0 coins
	Digitally signed by me
Transaction 1	**I am creating five electronnic coins: coin 1, coin 2, coin 3, coin 4, coin 5**
	My balance: coin 1, coin 2, coin 3, coin 4, coin 5
	Digitally signed by me

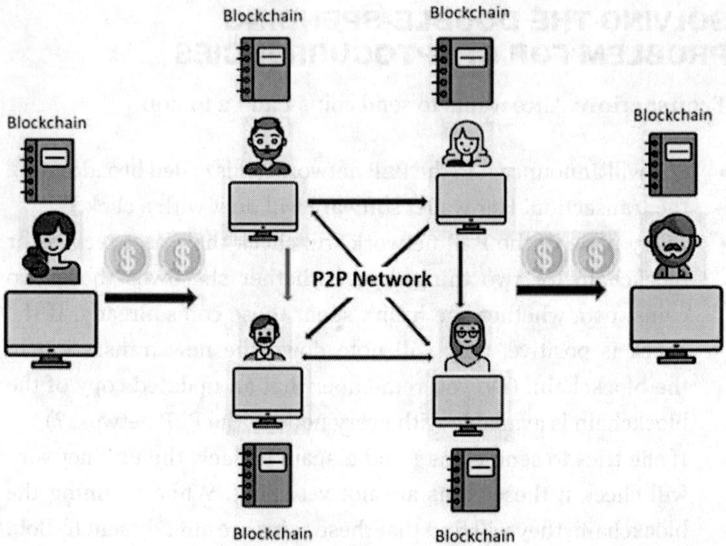

solving the double-spending problem and saved ourselves from many issues of centralization discussed in the previous chapters.

Note: The bitcoin blockchain doesn't track account balances.

We have solved two critical challenges for our newly created E-coin.

1. **Stealing:** No one can steal our money because the owner must digitally sign the transaction to spend money. And as we will see later, only the owner of the coins can produce a valid digital signature.
2. **Cheating:** No one can cheat or double-spend the same coins as everyone is watching. A blockchain is available with everyone in the P2P network that contains who owns what at any point in time.

You must be thinking why no one has produced these simple solutions. Cryptologists had suggested these solutions well before the invention of Bitcoin, and Satoshi himself used them. But there was another massive problem to solve if you wanted to create a distributed ledger system. This problem is infamously known as the 'problem of distributed consensus'. Satoshi Nakamoto solved this problem in a way that no one had thought of before him.

9 CONSENSUS

It is impossible to create a digital DMM without solving the problem of double-spending. And to solve the double-spending problem, we must solve the problem of decentralized consensus. Imagine that our E-coin network has 10 members who are running 10 E-coin nodes. Whenever someone does a transaction, they broadcast it to everyone. Everyone records it in their ledger. Since the ledger is not stored in one place, we call it distributed ledger, and because no party is in control, we call it a decentralized ledger. If Alice sends money to Bob through banks, they can check with banks whether the transaction is completed or not. But in the case of E-coin, they must check with every member. This is called a consensus-based system, as everyone has to agree on a single version of the truth.

PROBLEM OF DECENTRALIZED CONSENSUS

How can a group of people who don't have to disclose their true identities or trust each other agree on a single accurate version of the ledger when some are malicious?

What can prevent our E-coin users from deciding a single actual ledger state? One is *technical difficulties* like some of the members may be absent or offline, some may receive the transactions late, or some may not be able to respond because their node is not working. Cryptocurrency systems like Bitcoin can have millions of users.

Transactions are initiated from various parts of the world, and they reach different nodes at different speeds because of network issues, Internet connection speed and other factors. If every node records the transactions whenever it receives them, there will be thousands of conflicting ledgers containing different order of transactions. How can a user know which one is the true copy of the ledger?

The second obstacle is *dishonesty*. In a system with no central verifier, it's vital to ensure that nobody is cheating or trying to record a cheating transaction. There are four kinds of transactions from an ethical standpoint.

Authentic transaction: It is signed by the owner and contains the whole chain of ownership, which can link it to the first owner.
Valid transaction: It doesn't double-spend the same coins.
Unauthentic transaction: It steals others' money by copying their signature.
Invalid transaction: It defrauds others by giving them fake money (spending already spent coins).

Transactions which are authentic and valid should only be recorded in the ledger. Unauthentic transactions that try to steal others' funds are easily prevented because copying others' digital signature is impossible. The problem is created by transactions which are *authentic but invalid*. These transactions are intended to cheat others by *double-spending*. For simplicity's sake, we can call these 'cheating transactions'.

An example of a cheating transaction was given in the previous chapter where Alice double-spends -coins 1 and 2 on Jack. This is an authentic transaction signed by the owner, and it contains the chain of ownership to prove that she had acquired these coins from me. However, it is an invalid transaction because she has fooled Jack by paying fake coins. These coins are counterfeit because these are already spent on Bob.

It is also possible that some users collude with the majority of the users to defraud others. If this happens, loads of fake money will be created in the system. For example, here is how Alice can fool minority by conspiring with majority members of the E-coin network.

Alice has bribed Lexi, Peter, Murry and Don and told them not to record her payments. Silla and Tom are not online for the last two days. Jack is on a holiday trip. Bob and Lucy are present and maintaining their copy of the ledger honestly. When Alice sends E-coins 1 and 2 to Bob, it is recorded by only two members. Five members deliberately omit it. Three members couldn't record it due to technical reasons.

Therefore, there are *two conflicting versions* of ledgers.

> **False version:** There are five copies of the fraudulent ledger held by Alice and her malicious friends Lexi, Peter, Murry and Don. As per this ledger, Alice still owns E-coins 1 and 2.
> **Correct version:** Two true copies of the ledger are available with Bob and Lucy.

When Jack returns from the trip, he asks for a copy of the updated ledger. He gets five false copies and two true copies. Having no better option, he goes with the majority and accepts the faulty copy as the authentic version. Alice creates a cheating transaction and buys a mobile from Jack by spending counterfeit E-coins 1 and 2. Jack takes it because Alice still owns these coins as per his ledger. Alice and her friends again intentionally omit to record this new transaction. As a result, two fake coins are created in the system. If Alice continues to control more than half of the users, she can repeat her cheating transaction on every new joiner. All these users will be holding bags of fake money. And when they try to spend these coins, Alice and her team will reject their transactions. This kind of attack is called a 51 per cent attack.

SOLVING THE PROBLEM OF DECENTRALIZED CONSENSUS

Proofs exist which show that it is impossible to solve the problem of decentralized consensus. Byzantine generals problem and Fischer–Lynch–Paterson impossibility result are two of them. They proved that consensus is impossible even if a single node is faulty or malicious out of millions. The Genius of Satoshi Nakamoto lies in providing a practical solution to the problem of decentralized consensus. It is an elegant mix of economics and computer science. It is called 'proof of work'. We will apply the principles of POW to E-coin.

Solving the Problem of Dishonesty

If we know the identity of illicit users, we can punish them. We can ban them, report them to authorities or enforce penalties. But do you remember that there are no authorities in a decentralized system? There cannot be a person or group to implement rules and enforce punishments. Further, we *cannot* appoint an honest group of users as record keepers. It would lead to centralization; these people can be coerced to record malicious transactions or become corrupt. We need a different approach to inject honesty into the system. What if we can incentivize honest users instead of focusing on punishing malicious users?

We can create an incentive system based on three broad principles of human nature.

- Most of us act in our self-interest.
- Most of us want to get rewarded for our effort.
- If the benefit of protecting something is higher than the cost of destroying that thing, most of us will choose to protect that thing.

An Incentive System to Promote Honesty and Good Behaviour

1. A copy of the ledger is available to everyone, but not everyone can write in the ledger without putting *effort*. You must do *some work* or *incur some cost* to record transactions in the database.

2. But why would anyone volunteer to record transactions of others by spending out of their pocket? No one wants to do free work. We need to apply the *principle of reward:* Anyone who puts effort into recording transactions in the ledger will be rewarded with new E-coins.

3. One of the properties of sound money is 'scarcity'. Scarce things tend to be desirable and valuable. Similar to gold, there will be only a limited number of E-coins. New currencies can only be created when someone puts effort into recording authentic and valid transactions and get rewarded in E-coins. Since creating new E-coins is analogue to mining gold, we call these record keepers 'miners'.

4. How does this guarantee that the miners will act honestly? It doesn't guarantee honesty but makes it highly probable. If you can make more money by being honest than a cheater, you will prefer to be honest, assuming you wanted to make money by cheating in the first place.

5. Creating E-coin consumes a lot of electricity and computing power. If you want to make money as a miner, you will want those new coins as a reward to pay off your electricity and hardware cost.

6. Most of the miners will act in their self-interest. They would want to earn new coins, recover electricity costs and make a profit. Ultimately, every transaction will be verified by everyone, miners plus users. And the transactions which are approved by the majority only get into the ledger. Miners wouldn't like to record malicious transactions, as there is a high chance that others will reject them, and they would lose the opportunity to earn new E-coins.

7. Wouldn't the miners with criminal intent want to sabotage the system? Most of them wouldn't, as they would abide by the third principle of human nature. They are more likely to protect the system that provides them with a living.

Solving the Problem of Conflicting Ledgers

We cannot control the speed at which the users in the network initiate the transactions. But we can manage the rate at which they are recorded in each node's ledgers. To minimize the number of different ledger copies, we must do two things.

1. Slow the rate at which transactions are recorded. It will allow them to reach all or most of the nodes in the network. To achieve this, we record the transaction in batches or bundles. These bundles of transactions are called 'blocks'. The blocks are time-stamped and arranged in a chronological order forming the blockchain. Whenever new blocks are created, they are added to the already existing chain of blocks.

2. We should make the block-adding process deliberately tricky so that it is unlikely for more than one node to append a block simultaneously. We can achieve this by designing a cryptographic puzzle, which every miner will compete to solve. The miner who solves the puzzle first will get the chance to add the block and get new E-coins. Solving the puzzle must be dependent on luck. It must be impossible for a computer to solve the puzzle by analysing the past results, logic or shortcuts. The only way to solve the puzzle is to try every possible solution until the node hits the solution by luck. While the puzzle is tedious to solve, other members should easily verify its solution. This creates fairness in the block creation process. Further, there is no central authority that appoints miners. Anyone with a computer can become a miner.

Solving the puzzle proves that the miner has spent electricity and hardware cost. They are invested in it. Once the puzzle is solved, every miner in the network checks the solution, and if it is valid, they abandon working on the same block and add the block to their blockchain. In this way, every miner can maintain an exact copy of the blockchain. We can call this a consensus chain.

POW doesn't guarantee truth. It only provides *probable truth.* Once a transaction is added to a valid block, it is said to have been confirmed with one confirmation. When a new block is added to its top, it has two confirmations. The number of confirmations increases as new blocks are getting added. More the number of confirmations, more difficult it is to modify or delete your transaction from the blockchain. But there will *never be a final confirmation* which says that your transaction can't be replaced within the ledger. When two or more miners mine a block simultaneously, users will randomly pick one of these blocks and add it to their copy of the blockchain. Until the next block is mined, there will be more than one version of the blockchain. But once the block is mined and added to a specific version of the blockchain, others abandon their versions and accept the longest consensus chain (this chain is one block longer than others). This is called the Nakamoto consensus.

Let's consider an example: Alice sends E-coins 1 and 2 to Bob and buys a pair of shoes. Simultaneously, she creates a cheating transaction and spends the same coins on Jack to buy a mobile. There is no way for miners to spot which one of these is a cheating transaction as both of them are authentic and valid from a technical perspective. Therefore, these transactions can end up in two valid blocks mined by two different miners simultaneously. Any one of these blocks can become part of the consensus chain. Bob will lose his money if a block with the cheating transaction is added to the blockchain. Jack will lose money if the other block gets added. And in case of Bitcoin, this status can change for the following six blocks.

Competing versions of blockchain are usually resolved within two–three blocks; however, it is suggested to wait for six blocks. Therefore, the correct version of the ledger remains ambiguous for the following six blocks. Since it is practically impossible to change the ledger beyond six blocks, the correct version of the ledger probably exists before six blocks. The number of blocks required for ensuring a high probability of immutability depends on the difficulty with which blocks are mined. For example, a block in Bitcoin takes on average 10 minutes to mine, and the difficulty is adjusted automatically after every 2016 blocks to maintain the rate of block creation to on average 10 minutes. Therefore, we must decide the difficulty level we want for our E-coin.

There is no cryptographic protection for cheating transactions. The only defence is waiting for the original transaction to get a certain number of confirmations so that the probability of it getting replaced by a cheating transaction is infinitesimal. With this, we have completed the creation and implementation of E-coin. In the following chapters, we will dig deep into the technical aspects of blockchain and Bitcoin.

PART 2
Cryptography and Blockchain

10 HASH

The word 'cryptography' came from two Greek words: *kryptos* and *graphein*. *Kryptos* means 'hidden' or 'secret', and *graphein* means 'to write'. Hence, cryptography means 'secret writing'. It means tools, techniques and practices used for secure communication. Militaries, spies and intelligence agencies have used it to carry out secret missions. It would have been impossible to create the digital DMM of cryptocurrencies without advancements in cryptography. From signing a transaction to validating a block, everything depends on cryptography. Therefore, it is essential to understand the cryptography employed in creating and deploying cryptocurrencies. We will cover three crucial concepts of cryptography in the following three chapters.

1. Hash
2. Public and private keys
3. Digital signature

HASH

We know that different individuals have different fingerprints. A fingerprint is an identifier of a person. Similarly, hash identifies digital documents, including texts, audio, video and multimedia files.

Hash Function

It converts digital documents to a unique alphanumeric number by following a sequence of mathematical steps. This number is called 'the message digest' or 'hash'.

Hash Algorithm

You don't need to calculate hash manually, as the hash function can be automated by software.

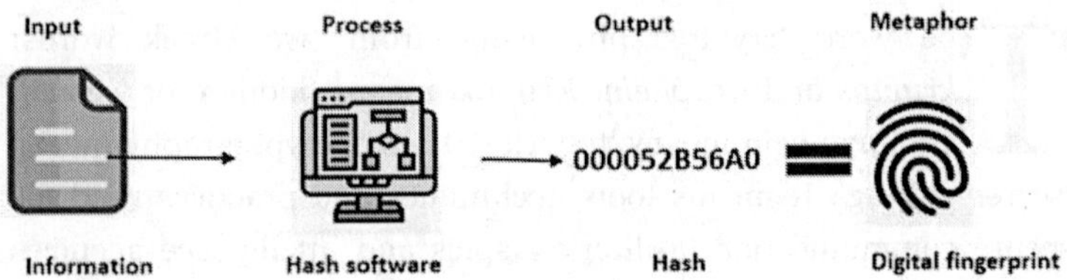

Importance of Hash

1. It is an identity proof of data: It helps to check whether a document is the same or altered during transmission without going through the details within the document.

2. Hash has a fixed length: Irrespective of the data size, hash has a fixed length of characters (usually 64 alphanumeric characters).

3. It hides the data: It proves that two documents are the same without revealing the details of two documents. It is practically impossible to know the input data from its hash.

Let's understand these three properties with an example. Assume you are a lawyer. A client has requested you to prepare a critical legal document by 15 August. This digital document is 5,000-page long. Today is 15 August, and you have finished your work. Your client is yet to make the payment. You don't want to send the document unless the payment is made. But you want to have proof that the work is completed on time to avoid future disputes. Hash algorithm can help you in this case.

1. You can hash the document and generate the hash number. For example, let's say the hash is a749a7dfabb21b034e25fb6bae9e617bc043e914d3dc964e50263eb3a8fca214

2. You can send a message to the client today and ask for payment. Include the hash number in the message.

Whenever the client makes the payment, you can hand over the document. How can the client verify that it is the same document which was prepared on 15 August? He has to copy–paste the content of the document in hash software. If he gets a hash a749a7dfabb21b034e25fb6bae9e617bc043e914d3dc964e50263eb3a8fca214, it proves that it is the same document because you have sent him this number on 15 August. If there is any dispute over the completion of work on time, you can prove that the work was completed on 15 August.

Cryptographic Hash Function

These functions must satisfy the five conditions mentioned below.

1. Always same: Same information always results in the same hash.

2. Going forward is easy: It should be easy to compute hash.

3. Going backward is not possible: Getting the input data from hash should not be possible.

Points 2 and 3 combined are called 'trapdoor functions'. Getting into the room is easy, but once you get in, you are trapped; you can't get out. The only way to get out is to try every possible input arrangement. It is called the 'brute force of the attack'.

4. Small change in data causes a substantial change in hash: Even if a single character changes in the input data, hash will change substantially. The new hash cannot be correlated to the old hash. This is called the 'avalanche effect'.

5. It is impossible to have the same hash for two different input data: This condition makes the cryptographic hash an identifier of digital things.

Examples of industry-standard cryptographic hash functions are MD5, BCRYPT and SHA256. Bitcoin blockchain uses the SHA256 hash function.

Hash Function	Example Hash
MD5	5f4dcc3b5aa765d61d8327deb882cf90
SHA1	5baa61e4c9b93f3f0682250b6cf8331b7ee68fd8
SHA256	5e884898da28047151d0e56f8dc6292773603d0d6aabbdd62a11ef721d1542d8

Note: In SHA256, SHA stands for Secure Hash Algorithm. In computer science, each character is four bits. SHA256 has 64 characters; hence, it has 64 × 4 = 256 bits. Therefore, it is called SHA256 hash.

TIME FOR A DEMO

Go to the following link using any browser other than Internet Explorer: https://andersbrownworth.com/blockchain/hash

This is a demo for SHA256 hash. Hence, any input you provide, you will get 64 characters. Play around and see how hash changes drastically, even if you change a single character in the input.

For example, let me type 'I am.' I got the following hash

Hash: afa497455f37b1c5502215a120fb275f10a6029b528bbab73a2e12f81bc53a1b

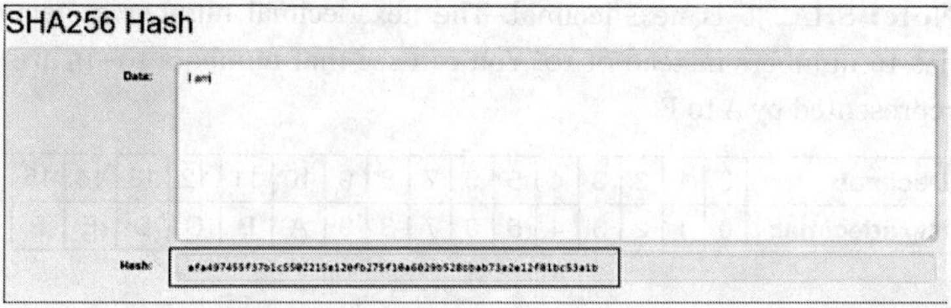

Let me change the capital case I to a small case i. This is the hash I got.

Hash: 7884f4b7cd3fffaf6924ed60742dfa9593fbc06818a3582aa7ed51a13c2b9e3c

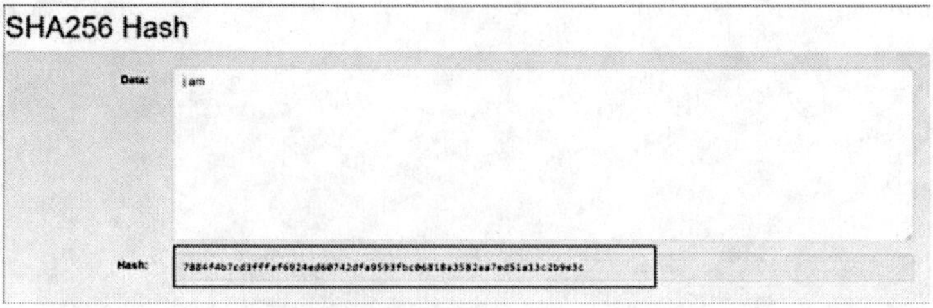

See how a slight change in the input caused a catastrophic change in hash. There is no way to link the changes to two hashes.

I copied the content of the whole Wikipedia page on war and peace, as presented below. I got 64 characters only. Even if you feed all the information in the world, it will give you 64 characters.

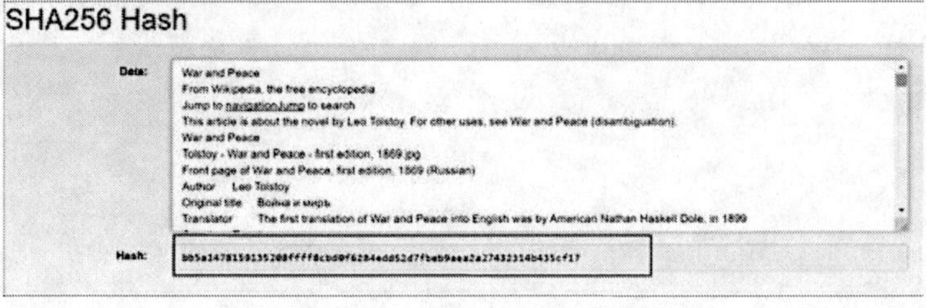

Note: SHA256 is hexadecimal. The hexadecimal number system has 16 numbers instead of 10. You can see that numbers 10–15 are represented by A to F.

Decimal:	0	1	2	3	4	5	6	7	8	9	10	11	12	13	14	15
Hexadecimal:	0	1	2	3	4	5	6	7	8	9	A	B	C	D	E	F

11 KEYS

Cryptography is all about encoding and decoding messages. Encoding a message is called encryption, whereas decoding is called decryption. The sender encodes the readable message into a jumbled text; the receiver decodes the messy text into a readable original message. The purpose is to prevent others from reading the message. The jumbled text is also called ciphertext.

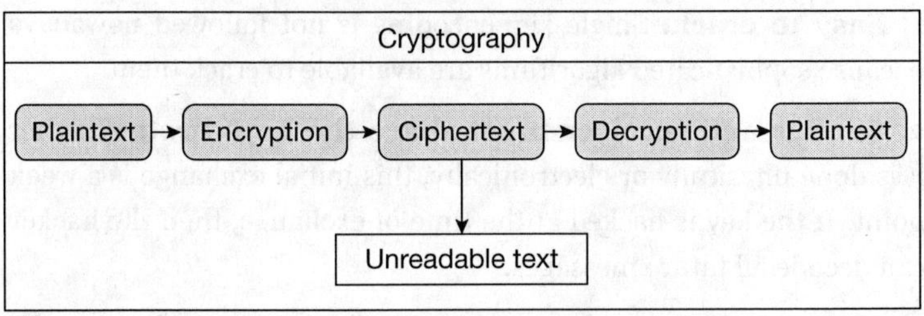

Coding and decoding are done using some logic. This logic is called the key.

There are two types of coding systems.

SYMMETRIC KEY CODING

Both encoding and decoding are done using a single key shared between sender and receiver. For example, Bob has sent an encrypted message to Murphy below. The key is known to both. They have used a simple key: Reverse. It means that the message is encoded by reversing the message. Once Murphy receives the ciphered message, he can decode it by reversing again.

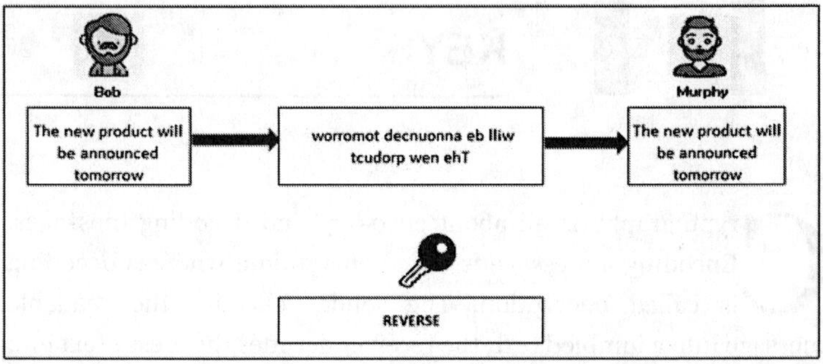

Problems with Symmetric Key Coding

1. Easy to crack: Single key encoding is not followed nowadays because sophisticated algorithms are available to crack them.

2. Sender and receiver must share the keys first: Whether it is done physically or electronically, this initial exchange is a weak point. If the key is hacked at the time of exchange, then the hacker can decode all future messages.

Cryptocurrencies use the asymmetric key system due to the shortcomings of the symmetric key system. Let's understand how the asymmetric key system works.

ASYMMETRIC KEY CODING

Encoding and decoding are done using separate keys.

Private key: As the name suggests, you keep it private.
Public key: You share this with the world.

If anyone wants to send you a message, they can use your public key to encode it. Once you receive the encoded message, you can decode it using your private key. Key pairs are generated using a mathematical scheme called elliptic curve digital signature algorithm (ECDSA), which is a robust algorithm used for Bitcoin.

Below you can see that Murphy has generated a public–private key pair. He has shared the public key with Bob. Bob encodes the message using Murphy's public key. And when Murphy receives the ciphered message, he can easily decode it using his private key.

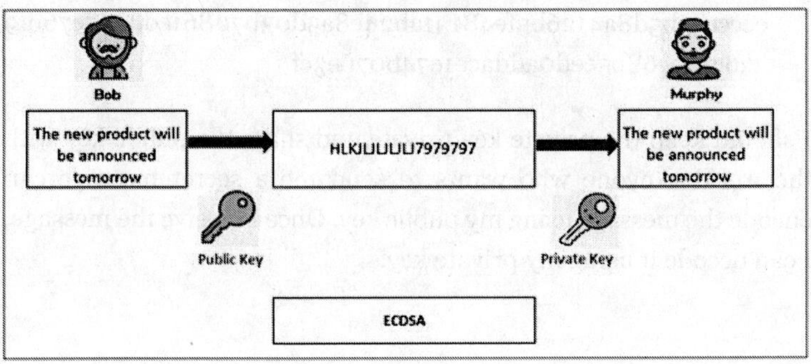

Since there is no way to know Murphy's private key from his public key, he doesn't have to worry about sharing the public key.

TIME FOR A DEMO

Go to the following link using any browser other than Internet Explorer: https://andersbrownworth.com/blockchain/public-private-keys/keys

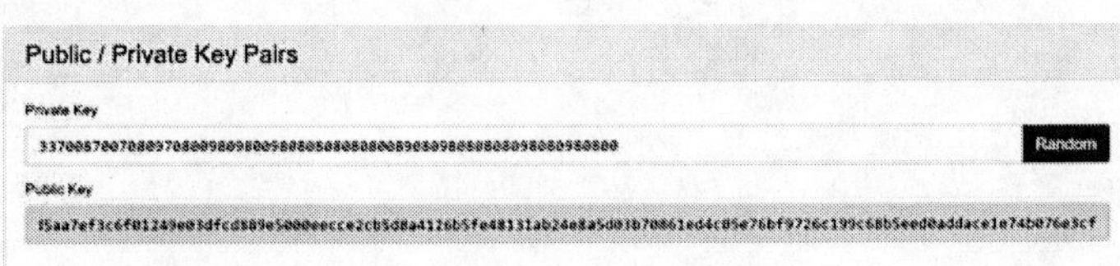

1. Type any random number in the private key field.

2. It will generate a public key.

Please make sure that the 'number for the private key is large, and you type it randomly'. This reduces the chance of two people having the same public–private key to almost zero.

For example, I have generated below private and public keys.

> **Private key:** 33700870070809708009809800980808 08080 8008908098080808098080980800
> **Public key:** 04db8b01f65d5aa7ef3c6f01249e03dfcd889e5000 eecce2cb5d8a4126b5fe48131ab24e8a5d03b70861ed4c05e76bf9 726c199c68b5eed0addace1e74b076e3cf

I should keep the private key private and share the public key with the world. Anyone who wants to send me a secret message can encode the message using my public key. Once I receive the message, I can decode it using my private key.

12 SIGNATURE

A signature is a way to approve or authenticate something. For example, If I see your signature on a document, it means that you, the owner of the signature, have approved it.

Cryptocurrency networks have many participants, and transactions are visible to everyone. Hence, anonymity is crucial. Participants must remain anonymous to protect themselves from coercion, threat and other criminal attacks. The challenge is to:

1. Create an unforgeable signature.

2. Create a signature that proves your authentication without disclosing your identity to anyone.

Both challenges are solved by digital signature.

DIGITAL SIGNATURE

Private keys are used to create digital signatures. And public keys are used for verifying the signature.

How Does This Work?

You can encode a message using your private key, and people can decode it using your public key. It is the exact opposite process we had learned in the public–private key section. The encoded message (ciphertext) can work as a digital signature. If others can decode your signature using your public key, only you have created the signature.

Logic

1. Public–private key pairs are linked mathematically.

2. The chance of two people having the same public–private key pair is close to zero.

Hence, it is indisputable that one who owns the public key must also be the owner of a private key. Let's take an example. Suppose Bob wants to send a message to Murphy. Bob can sign it digitally so that Murphy can be sure that Bob authenticated it.

Bob can follow this process (refer to the picture below):

1. He will encode the message using his private key. He will get a ciphertext, for example, N02HLJJLH1083LKKLK. This encoded text is his digital signature.

2. He will send the message and the signature to Murphy.

Murphy can validate the message and signature as follows:

He will use **Bob's** public key to decode the signature or ciphertext.

1. If he can decode, only the public key owner has signed it through his private key. (Point 1 in the below picture)

2. If the decoded message matches with the original message, then the message is not altered or tampered with on the way. (Point 2 in the below picture)

There is one issue. If Bob wants to send a large document, his digital signature would be large. To prevent this, he can hash the document and then encrypt the hash to generate the digital signature.

Bob can follow this process (refer to the picture below):

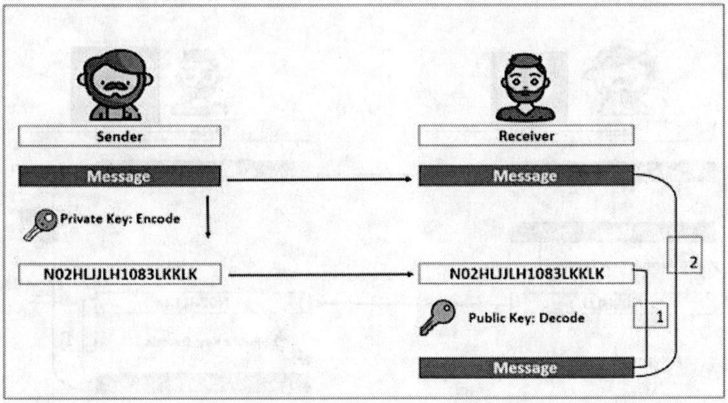

1. He will hash the message using a hash algorithm.

2. He will encode the hash using the private key. He will get shortened ciphertext, for example, NO2HLJJ. This is his digital signature.

3. He will send the message and the signature to Murphy.

Murphy can validate the message and signature as follows:

He will use Bob's public key to decode the signature (ciphertext) and get the hash value.

1. If he can decode, only the owner of the public key has signed it through his private key. (Point 1 in the below picture)

Then he will get the hash value of Bob's message by running the same hash algorithm.

2: If the signature's hash matches with the original message's hash, then the message is not altered or tampered with on the way. (Point 2 in the below picture)

Private key + Transaction = Digital signature Verification = Transaction + Public key + Digital signature = Valid/Invalid

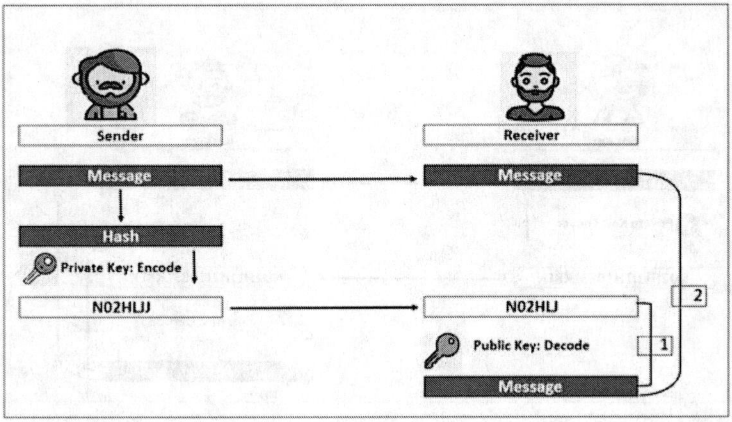

Some Benefits of Digital Signature

Following are some benefits of digital signature:

- **Security:** There is no way to identify the private key from the public key. Hence, no one can generate a digital signature except the private key holder.
- **Anonymity:** It can be proved mathematically that the digital signature is done by the person who owns the public–private key pair. You are hidden behind your public key. You need not prove your true identity to anyone.
- **Non-repudiation:** Once you receive a digitally signed document, the sender cannot prove that he didn't sign the document.
- **Tamper proof:** Even a minute change in the message will change the digital signature. Hence, it is not possible to tamper with the message.
- **Valid only for that specific message:** It is valid for only that message. No one can copy and use it for any other documents.

TIME FOR A DEMO

Go to the following link using any browser other than Internet Explorer: https://andersbrownworth.com/blockchain/public-private-keys/signatures

Type a message. Enter your private key and click on the sign. It will create a digital signature. For example, I had created the below public–private key pair in the previous chapter.

> **Private key:** 33700870070809708009809800980808080 80 0089080980808080980809808 00
> **Public key:** 04db8b01f65d5aa7ef3c6f01249e03dfcd889e5000eecce2cb5d8a4126b5fe48131ab24e8a5d03b70861ed4c05e76bf9726c199c68b5eed0addace1e74b076e3cf

Let me enter some messages and sign the message using my private key.

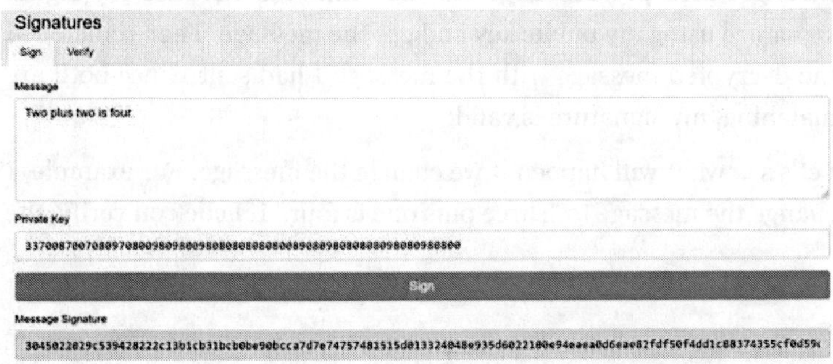

Here is my digital signature for this particular message:
3045022029c539428222c13b1cb31bcb0be90bcca7d7e74757481515d013324048e935d6022100e94eaea0d6eae82fdf50f4dd1c88374355cf0d59d5dcc0775992917eab674635

I will broadcast this message and my digital signature to the P2P network. How would they verify my signature?

Let's go to the 'Verify' tab. They can verify my message using my public key and signature.

In this demo, if the screen turns green, my signature is valid.

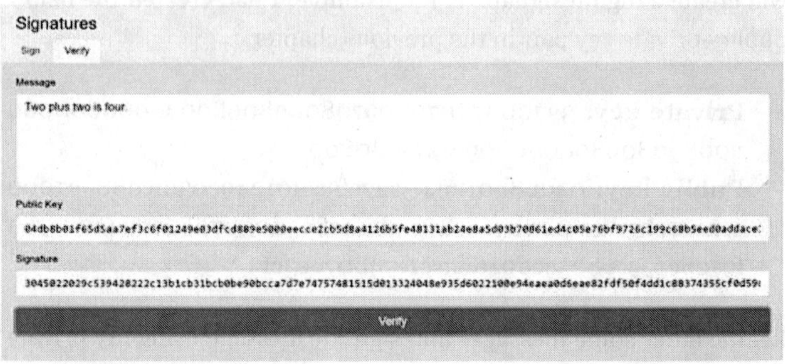

Background processing: The algorithm has decoded my digital signature using my public key and got the message. Then it matched the decrypted message with the message I had sent. Since both are matching, my signature is valid.

Let's see what will happen if we change the message. For example, I change the message to 'Three plus one is four.' If I click on verify, the

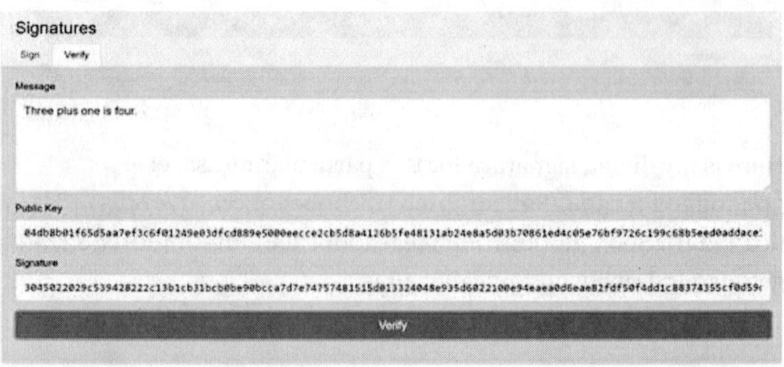

screen turns red. It indicates that the message has been altered. My signature is not valid for this modified message.

In this demo, if the screen turns green, my signature is valid.

Background processing: The algorithm has decoded my digital signature using my public key and got the message. Then it matched the decrypted message with the message I had sent. Since both are matching, my signature is valid.

Let's see what will happen if we change the message. For example, I change the message to 'Three plus one is four.' If I click on 'Verify', the screen turns red. It indicates that the message has been altered. My signature is not valid for this modified message.

13 BLOCKCHAIN

Blockchain is a distributed, decentralized and immutable *ledger*. Let's breakdown each of these aspects one by one.

BLOCKCHAIN IS A LEDGER

A ledger is nothing but a chronological log of transactions. Whenever we think of financial ledgers, bank accounts come to mind. For example, I have an opening bank balance of $1,000. I have made transactions; now my closing account balance is $900. This kind of model is natural to us. Accounting ledgers are also structured in the same manner. This is called account-based model. Some cryptocurrencies like Ether are based on this model, whereas cryptocurrencies like bitcoin are based on a transaction-based model.

BLOCKCHAIN IS A DISTRIBUTED LEDGER

It is important to distinguish between distributed database, distributed ledger and blockchain.

> **Distributed database:** It has more than one updated copy of data saved in multiple locations. If data in one location gets destroyed, it is preserved in another location. Further, the access speed increases as users can connect to their nearest database. The goal of distributed database is to 'provide efficient, low-cost

services while preventing single point of failure'. For example, Google, Amazon and Facebook use distributed databases located around the world.

Distributed ledger: Similar to distributed databases, a copy of data is available with *all* the nodes operated by independent users. What distinguishes distributed ledger from distributed database is that the former is a *consensus-based system,* while the latter is not. If someone wants to write something in their copy, all the nodes must *verify and approve it.* For example, Bitcoin's distributed ledger follows POW to arrive at consensus on the state of ledger. Further distributed ledgers are protected by high level of cryptography.

Blockchain: It is a specific kind of Distributed ledger. All blockchains are distributed ledgers. *But not all distributed ledgers are Blockchains.* There are distributed ledgers that don't record information in a *chain of blocks.* Therefore, blockchains are a *specific kind* of distributed ledger where data is recorded in blocks.

BLOCKCHAIN IS A DECENTRALIZED LEDGER

Doesn't distributing a ledger make it decentralized? The answer is 'No'. Here, the centre means a point of control, a point of power or a point of exclusive rights—*a matter of authority.* Decentralization means distribution of ownership in the ledger, not distribution of copies.

Example: Google Sheets

Google Sheets allows many participants to edit and modify the content concurrently. It a *distributed ledger,* as a copy of the sheet is available to everyone. Assume that we are a group of 10,000 participants using this ledger to record our transactions. Isn't Google Sheets a decentralized ledger? To answer this question, all participants must ask: Do we have the right to change the programming and design of Google Sheets without the approval of Google? Do we have the right to stop distributing Google Sheets if we want? Do we have the right to decide how it will be marketed? Can we prevent Google if it decides to stop this product? Can we prevent Google from modifying and deleting data? I hope each one of you has answered 'No' because Google *owns* and *controls* Google Sheets. But Google Sheets can be considered a decentralized ledger if it is available as an open-source software and there is no hierarchy of authority within our 10,000 members.

BLOCKCHAIN IS AN IMMUTABLE LEDGER

Let's understand the specific kind of distributed ledger technology (DLT) used in blockchain.

Blocks: Blocks are groups of transactions.

The hash value of each block is dependent on its previous block. Since all blocks are dependent on their earlier blocks to the genesis block, any change in one block changes the block hash of all the subsequent blocks up to the present block. Blockchains are practically tamperproof, as no one can change data without getting noticed. Once others see that a specific blockchain is altered, they ignore it as invalid. Therefore, a chain of blocks makes blockchain an immutable record of facts. Blocks are connected through hash, which is supersensitive to atomic changes.

Let's create a simple blockchain to understand the significance of hash in connecting the blocks.

Creating a Simple Blockchain

Step 1: Assume that we have data in four blocks: Block 0, Block 1, Block 2 and Block 3. Block 0 is called the genesis block. This is the first block in the blockchain.

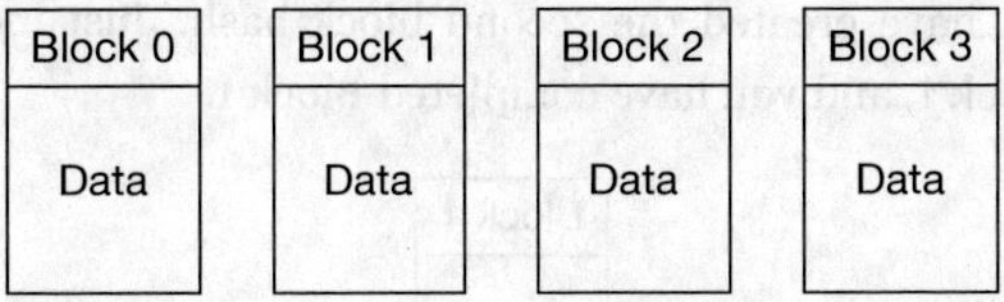

Step 2: Create the fingerprint of the first block; generate a hash for the data contained in Block 0.

The completed Block 0 will include its hash. Hence, Block 0 would look like as follows.

Step 3: Generate a hash for the data contained in Block 1.

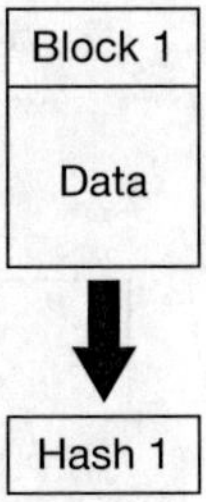

Great! You have created the second block hash. Just include this hash in Block 1, and you have completed Block 1.

Wait! You have finished two blocks, but are they linked? No. The foundation of a blockchain is dependent on blocks. We need to create a chain of dependent blocks.

Step 4: Let's correct our mistake. We must link Block 0 and Block 1. To do this, include the previous block hash 'Hash 0' in Block 1.

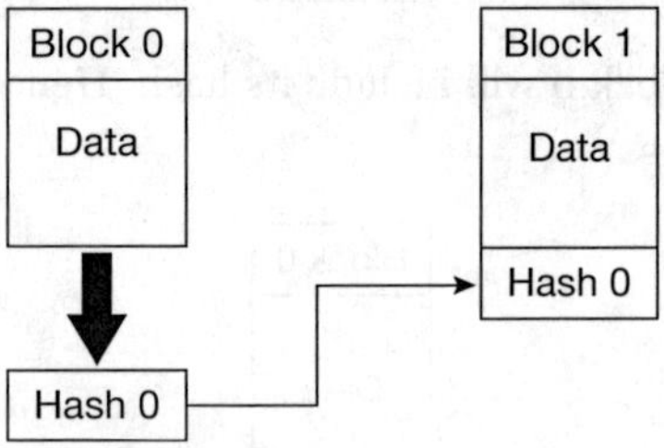

Step 5: Generate the hash for Block 1. Block 1 includes data + hash of the previous block (Hash 0).

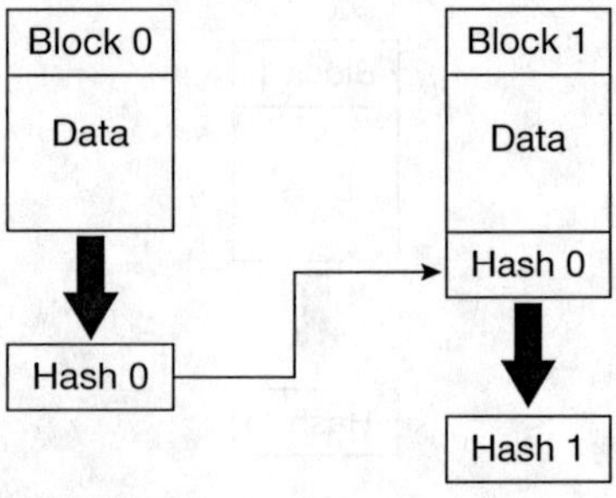

The completed Block 1 will include its hash (Hash 1). Hash 0 is already included. It will look like this:

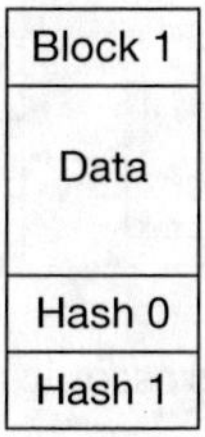

Now, you have connected the two blocks successfully.

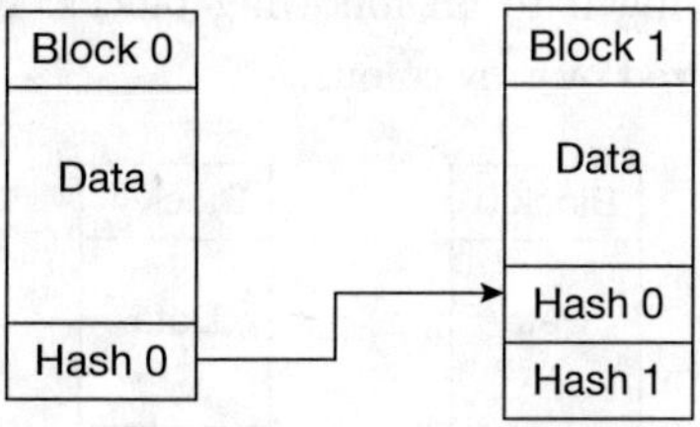

Step 6: Link Blocks 2 and 3 in the same manner.

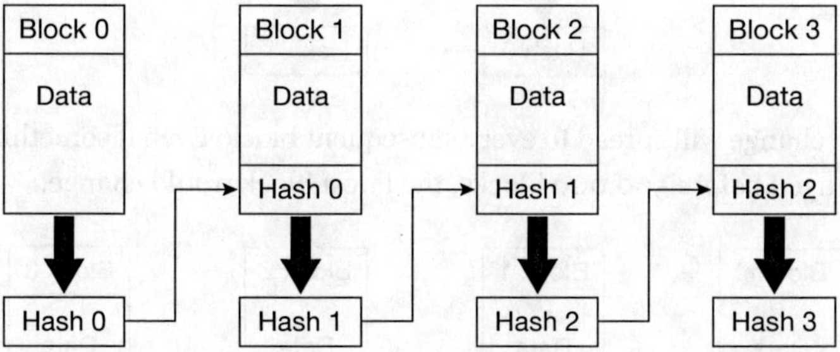

Congratulations! You have created a rudimentary blockchain. All the blocks are linked now by a hash chain.

Let's stop and consider why linking with hash makes blockchain challenging to tamper with. It's because of the avalanche effect of hash. Even a tiny change in a document creates a catastrophic shift

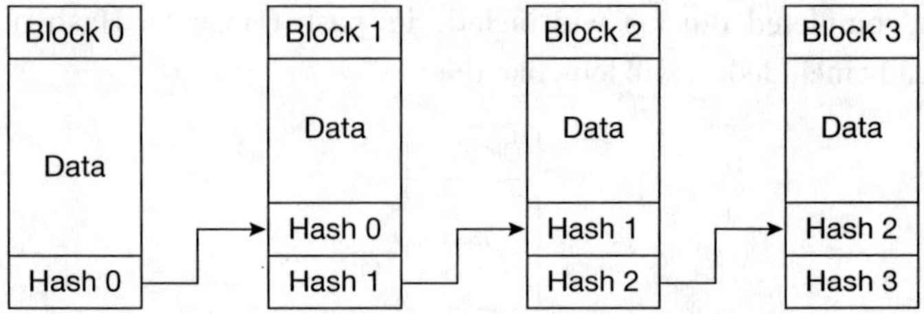

in hash. For example, any microscopic change in the data in Block 0 will change its hash. This change is contagious. It will spread to the next block. The next block will transmit the change to its subsequent neighbour, extending it to all following blocks. For visualization, change is represented by grey colour.

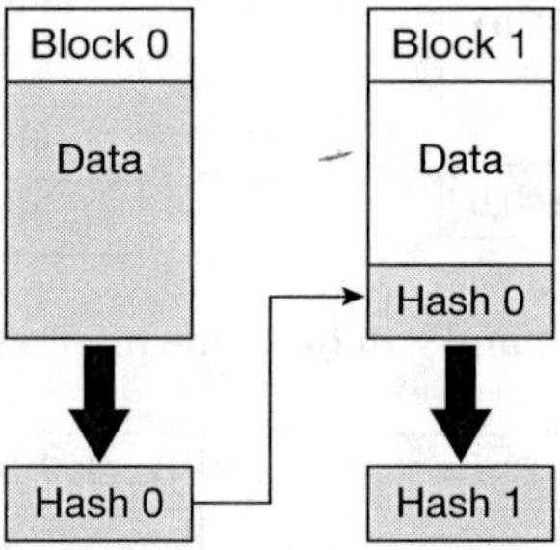

The change will spread to every subsequent block. Even if something changed before 500,000 blocks, the latest block would change.

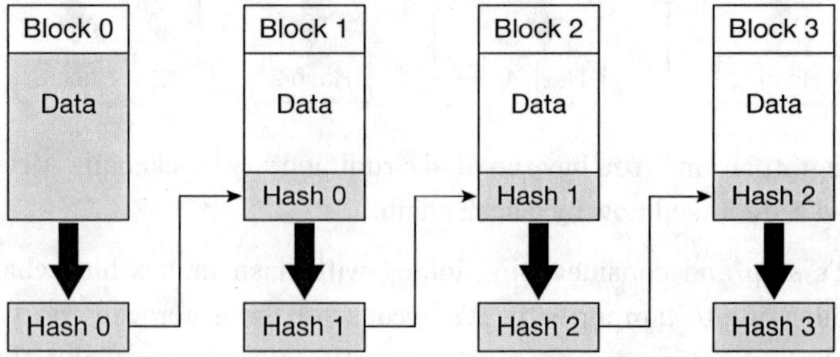

See how the change has affected all the subsequent blocks.

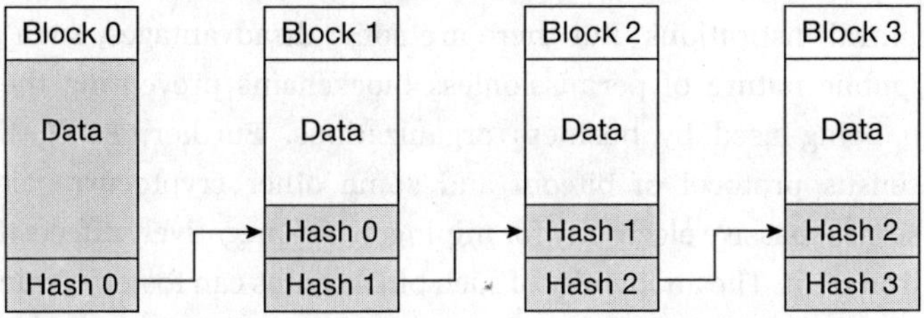

Suppose any modifications happen in any of the past blocks. In that case, you will notice the tampering just by looking at the hash of the latest block.

TYPES OF BLOCKCHAIN

The degree of decentralization is different for different situations. We need a completely decentralized blockchain for cases where many people are involved who don't trust each other. These kinds of blockchains are called public or permissionless blockchains. For example, it can add value wherever there is a shared system where trust and transparency are required: banking system, government systems, elections, supply chain of goods and services for public benefits, donations tracking, property records of citizens, criminal records, etc. However, a partially decentralized private or consortium blockchain is suitable for business organizations.

Public or Permissionless Blockchains

It is entirely decentralized. Anyone can join the network without anyone's permission. All the computers in the network have their copy of the ledger. They can update the ledger efficiently by using consensus protocols like POW or proof of stake (POS). It removes the dependency on central authorities and eliminates the need for trust. It creates transparency, provides solid security, protects privacy and empowers the public by shifting control from the hands of central institutions. But there are some disadvantages, such as the public nature of permissionless blockchains preventing them from being used by business organizations. Further, POW, the consensus protocol of bitcoin and some other cryptocurrencies, consumes massive electricity for mining, which negatively affects the environment. The anonymity of such blockchains can foster criminal activities.

Examples: Bitcoin, Ethereum and Solana

Private Blockchains

Only a single organization maintains and controls the blockchain. It offers partial decentralization and uses cryptography and distributed ledger within the organization. Participants are not anonymous. Only authorized people can join and work in the network. The ledger is protected from getting hacked; there is no single point of failure, data cannot be tampered. The system doesn't slow down as there are limited nodes. It doesn't require mining or POW to reach a consensus. But these blockchains are not genuinely decentralized, and centralized nodes make the last call; hence, trust is involved. Since there are only a few nodes, the security isn't good. More than 51 per cent of malicious users can modify data.

Examples: Multichain and Blockstack

Consortium Blockchains

Also known as federated blockchains, these provide a better solution to organizations' needs where they can use public and private blockchain features. Organizations can decide which data should be shared and what should be kept confidential. It is more decentralized than private blockchains managed by more than one organization. It is not open to the public, as only consortium members can participate in the blockchain. These blockchains don't require mining or POW to reach consensus. But these are less secure and transparent than public blockchains.

Examples: Hyperledger, Corda and Ripple

PART 3
Bitcoin

14 BITCOIN

Bitcoin is the first, most valuable cryptocurrency globally. The total value of the existing number of bitcoins was around $1.3 trillion when I started writing this book.[1] It was worth 20 per cent more in April 2021 when one bitcoin traded around $64,000.

Conventions: Bitcoin is a currency as well as a monetary system. The crypto community uses the terms 'Bitcoin' with a capital B to refer to the system and 'bitcoin' with the small case b to refer to the currency.

The DMM of Bitcoin has three elements: a decentralized currency called bitcoin or BTC, a decentralized network called bitcoin P2P network and a decentralized ledger called the bitcoin blockchain (Figure 14.1).

BITCOIN

We can understand the bitcoin currency at six different levels. It is the *world's first digitally scarce, decentralized, borderless, open-access and censorship-resistant electronic cash* at the user level. At the same time, *it is just a digital file* stored in the bitcoin blockchain at

1 Shomik Sen Bhattacharjee, 'Crypto Market Has Shed More Than $1 Trillion in Market Cap since November, Bitcoin Marks Six-Month Low', 24 January 2022, https://gadgets.ndtv.com/cryptocurrency/news/bitcoin-price-btc-cryptocurrency-market-crash-usd-1-trillion-coinmarketcap-2726233#:~:text=In%20fact%2C%20according%20to%20CoinMarketCap,crore)%20over%20the%20same%20period

Figure 14.1 Bitcoin Money Model

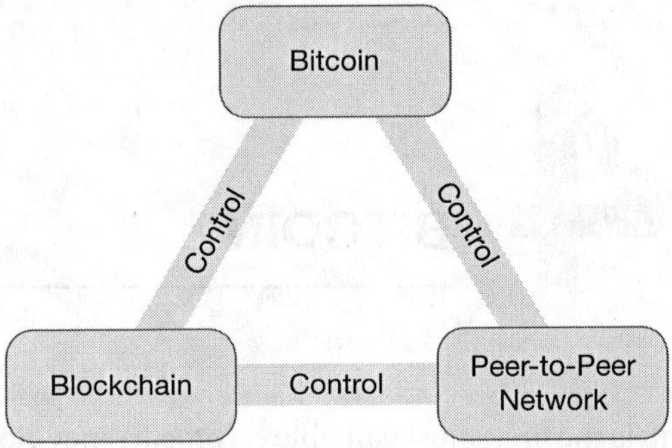

the database level. At the protocol level, *it is an unspent transaction output (UTXO)* defined by the bitcoin protocol. If you think from the software level, *it is a UTXO expressed in a coding language*. At a hardware level, *it is just a pattern of electric pulses* stored in computer memory and transmitted through computer networks. Finally, at the security level, *it is a digitally signed amount* that is sent from a public key to another public key, keeping the users pseudonymous.

BITCOIN P2P NETWORK

It is a decentralized and permissionless network of interconnected computers. Each node in the P2P network runs the *Bitcoin client software* to connect and transact in bitcoin. It is open access, as no permission is required to join the network. The network also stores and maintains the bitcoin blockchain. It uses POW consensus protocol to resolve the problem of conflicting versions of blockchain.

BITCOIN BLOCKCHAIN

The bitcoin blockchain is a linked list of digital files that contain bitcoin transactions. It is based on the UTXO model instead of the account-based model. The current size of its blockchain is around 300 GB. It is the most secure blockchain existing as of today.

A THIRD KIND OF MONEY

Dol you remember that in the second chapter, we had discussed two types of monetary media within TMM?

1. Token money: Coins and notes, typically known as physical currencies

2. Ledger money or digital money: Money as a ledger account balance, such as a balance in your bank account

Bitcoin is neither or both to some extent. To understand what it means, let's compare their key attributes.

Token Money

- All units of money are fungible. A $1 note is equivalent to any other $1 note.
- Coins are valid if they are authentic. Any coin or note produced by the mint of the central bank is valid.
- Ownership is not tracked.
- Spending the coin doesn't render it dead or useless.

Ledger Money

- It stores a list of accounts and balances.
- All units of money are fungible.
- Three conditions must be satisfied to spend money: You must own the money, have sufficient balance and authorize the transaction. Else the transaction will be invalid.
- Ownership is tracked.

BITCOIN

Here are some peculiar attributes of bitcoin:

- It doesn't have any concept of account balances. It doesn't store and track your bitcoin balance. (This makes it different from ledger money.)

- Every bitcoin is unique. Bitcoins *may not* be fungible. (This makes it different from token and ledger money.)
- Once you spend a bitcoin, that bitcoin is dead and can't be spent further. Therefore, you can use a bitcoin only once. (This makes it different from both token and ledger money.)
- Three conditions must be satisfied to spend money: You must own the bitcoins, have enough bitcoins and authorize the transaction. Else the transaction will be invalid. (This is the same as ledger money.)
- New bitcoins are created by *mining* and transferred to miners. Mining is when the coins are minted, and you must show that it is minted somewhere in the past. Therefore, to spend a bitcoin, *you must provide a chain of ownership* that goes back to the miner. (While the process of mining is like minting physical coins, the chain of ownership is similar to ledger money.)

Therefore, you can notice that bitcoins are a different kind of money which has some similarities with token and ledger money. Here are some interesting questions, the answers to which lie in bit

coin transactions. If once you spend a bitcoin, it is dead, then how can it have a history of ownership? How can it reach me if my previous owners have already spent it? Where are the bitcoins saved if the bitcoin blockchain doesn't have any account balance concept? If I don't have an account, how can I own a bitcoin? What does owning a bitcoin mean? We will tackle with these questions in the next chapter.

15 TRANSACTIONS

A transaction is the transfer of ownership of money. As you will see, bitcoins are born, live, die and even get killed, like human beings, which happen through transactions. But before we dive deep into transactions, we must understand Bitcoin addresses. Bitcoin doesn't require you to disclose your real identity. Therefore, we use our public keys. Further, we shorten the public key by hashing it. We use this address to send, receive and own a bitcoin. Please don't make a mistake thinking of it as an account number.

BITCOIN TRANSACTIONS

There are two kinds of transactions: coinbase and spend. While coinbase transactions create new bitcoins via mining, spend transactions use already mined bitcoins. For example, in the below screenshot, Tx ID 1 is a coinbase transaction where Bob has mined 50 fresh bitcoins.

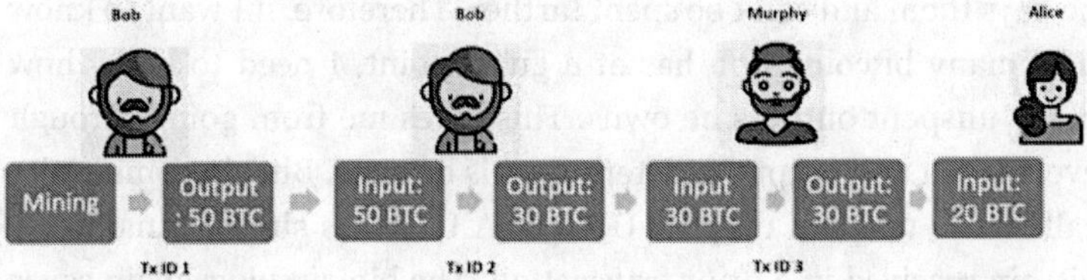

INPUTS AND OUTPUTS

Every transaction needs to specify where bitcoins are coming in and where bitcoins are going out. These are called inputs and outputs, respectively. By including the outputs or previous transactions as the input of the current transaction, we create a transaction chain. Each and every bitcoin can be traced back to its origin through the transaction chain.

For example:

In Tx ID 1,

Where are 50 bitcoins coming in (inputs)? Mining

Where are 50 bitcoins going out (outputs)? Bob's address

In Tx ID 2

Where are 50 bitcoins coming in (inputs)? Bob's address

Where are 30 bitcoins going out (outputs)? Murphy's address

In Tx ID 3

Where are 30 bitcoins coming in (inputs)? Murphy's address

Where are 30 bitcoins going out (outputs)? Alice's address

UTXO

Let's consider Tx ID 1, the first transaction. It has created an output of 50 BTC sent to Bob's address. These bitcoins remain unspent until Bob spends them in Tx ID 2. They are considered spent once he pays them and can't be spent further. Therefore, if I want to know how many bitcoins Bob has at a given point, I need to know how many unspent outputs he owns. This saves me from going through every input and output to determine his balance. Bitcoin community calls these unspent outputs UTXOs. A UTXO is simply a name for bitcoin received in a prior transaction. The bitcoin blockchain saves UTXOs in a unique database called LevelDB. The set of UTXOs is called 'chainstate'. The value of chainstate is the total value of bitcoin available at any time.

DEAD AND REBORN

Each UTXO is unique. We can identify a UTXO by transaction ID, which is nothing but the transaction hash and an index number. The output dies after it is spent, giving birth to new UTXOs of equal value. It is akin to throwing a bunch of coins into a machine that melts them and mints new coins of any denomination you want. Technically, once a UTXO is spent, it is taken out of LevelDB and replaced by new UTXOs created in the transaction. The complete set of UTXOs increases when people send bitcoins from one address to many and decreases when bitcoins are sent from many addresses to one address. A transaction can combine one or more UTXOs as inputs and pay as one or more UTXOs as outputs.

For example, look at the three transactions below. Tx ID 1 created a new UTXO of 50 BTC. Its unique ID is UTXO 1(1). The first one refers to a transaction ID, and the 1 in the bracket refers to the index. At this point, there are 50 BTC but only 1 UTXO in the chainstate. In transaction 2, Bob spends UTXO 1(1) of 50 BTC on Murphy and Alice. As a result, UTXO (1) is removed from chainstate, and two new outputs, UTXO 2(1) of 30 BTC and UTXO 2(2) of 20 BTC, are added. After the second transaction, there are 50 BTC but 2 UTXOs. Murphy and Alice decided to transfer their bitcoins to Lindy, running a non-profit organization for women empowerment. In transaction 3, they added their UTXOs and created UTXO 3(1) of 50 BTC for Lindy. Their UTXOs are replaced by UTXO 3(1) in the chain state. At this point, there is again only one UTXO and 50 BTC in the chainstate.

Note: The owner must digitally sign every transaction. In transaction 3, Murphy and Alice both need to sign the transaction as they own the UTXOs spent.

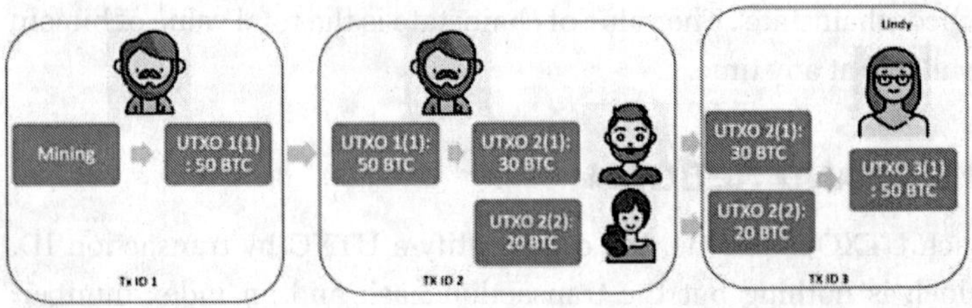

Your Bitcoin Core software downloads the UTXO set and keeps it updated. In the below picture, you can see the UTXO set or chainstate.

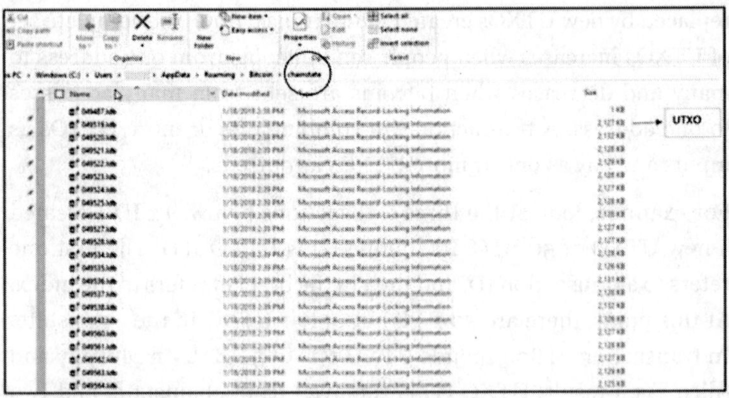

CHANGE

A UTXO cannot be spent in fractions. It must be spent as a whole. Inputs = output. This is like the debit = credit rule of double-entry accounting. All transactions must follow input value = output value. If you have a UTXO of 25 BTC, but you want to send 20 BTC to your friend, you must create two outputs:

UTXO 1: 20 BTC to your friend
UTXO 2: 5 BTC to yourself

This is called change. It is like buying a $25 pizza when you have a $20 bill and asking for a $5 change.

TRANSACTION FEES

If you want your BTC to be transferred soon, you need to pay some fees to miners. However, it is not mandatory to pay fees. For the above example, you create two outputs and leave some BTC to miners:

Output 1: 20 BTC to your friend
Output 2: 4.95 BTC to yourself
Balance: 0.05 BTC balance is assumed to be the fees you have decided to pay to the miners

TRANSACTION VALIDATION (WARNING! GEEK STUFF)

Whenever you want to spend a bitcoin, you must authenticate the transaction. A straightforward way to do this is to digitally sign the transaction using your private key and broadcast the signed transaction along with your public key. Everyone in the network can validate the transaction by verifying your signature using your public key.

But Bitcoin does it a little differently. Instead of signing the transaction, you need to send two scripts: SigScript and PkScript.

SigScript

It is also known as ScriptSig. This script includes your digital signature and public key. It can prove that you own the specific UTXOs you are trying to spend as the inputs. It looks something like this:

```
<sig>
<pubKey>
```

PkScript

It is also known as ScriptPubkey. This script includes the address of the receiver. It aims to lock the bitcoin in the receiver's name so that only they can spend them. Therefore, PkScript is called locking script, and SigScript is called unlocking script. It looks like this:

OP_DUP
OP_HASH
<pubkeyHash>
OP_EQUALVERIFY
OP_CHECKSIG

Concept note: A script is nothing but a set of instructions. Bitcoin scripting language was kept intentionally simple by Satoshi Nakamoto. You don't have to be a programmer to understand the logic behind the script. <> refers to data, and codes with OP are operations.

Example: Look at the input of transaction 10 below. Bob is trying to spend the UTXO of transaction 9. We will see how the Bitcoin scripts help us verify this transaction's authenticity.

We need to check whether Bob is eligible to spend the input UTXO 9(1) included in Tx ID 10. He has provided two scripts along with the input UTXO—SigScript of the current transaction and PkScript of the previous transaction. Once Bob initiates the transaction, the Bitcoin software running in the mining machines, PCs and mobiles of millions of users does this: It concatenates PkScript and SigScript and runs the scripts together.

Look at the below picture. On the left side, you see the scripts, and on the right side, you see how it runs. Consider the right side a stack which is empty initially. We will push items on the top from the left side to the bottom right side. Then we will follow the steps from bottom to top. Whenever an OP code is moved to the right, it operates on whatever items sit beneath it.

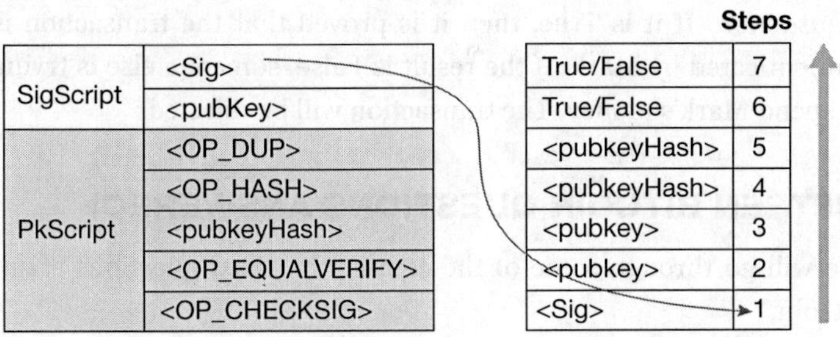

1. <sig> of Bob is pushed to the bottom. This is his signature for *the current transaction.*

2. <pubKey> of Bob is pushed on top of that. This is his public key for *the current transaction.*

3. OP_DUP is pushed above <pubKey>. It creates a duplicate of the public key provided for *the current transaction.*

4. OP_HASH is pushed to the top of the stack. It creates a hash of the public key provided in *the current transaction.*

5. <publickeyHash> is pushed to the top of the stack. It is the hash of the public key of Bob provided in the output of *the previous transaction by the previous owner.*

6. OP_EQUALVERIFY is pushed to the top of the stack. It verifies whether the current and previous transactions' public key hashes are equal. If equal, it shows TRUE. It proves that UTXO 9(1) of the previous transaction was indeed sent to Bob by the previous owner Lindy. The chain of ownership from the previous to the current transaction is demonstrated. The stack empties all the verified items leaving only <sig> and <pubKey>. Instead, if the result is false, then the processing stops, and the transaction is rejected. It means that Bob is trying to spend a UTXO he does not own.

7. Only if step 6 is true, step 7 is executed. OP_CHECKSIG is pushed to the top of the stack. It uses the public key used in the *current transaction* to verify the digital signature of Mark for the *current transaction*. If it is True, then it is proved that the transaction is authenticated by Mark. If the result is False, someone else is trying to spend Mark's money. The transaction will be rejected.

FIFTEEN BITCOIN QUESTIONS ANSWERED!

We will go through some of the commonly asked questions about bitcoin.

1. Why Does Bitcoin Use Scripts?

Scripts provide flexibility to construct a transaction. For example, we can create scripts that require two or more private keys to spend a UTXO.

2. What Exactly Is a Bitcoin?

It is the same as asking what exactly USD is. Well, USD is a currency that comes in different denominations. A USD can be a $500 bill or a $1 note or a few cents. Similarly, bitcoin is a currency that comes in different UTXOs. While each bitcoin can be divided into 100 million units called satoshis, fiat currency can't be divided and transacted at this level. A UTXO is nothing but a customized collection of satoshis. For example, if you have one bitcoin, you can send two UTXOs of 50 million satoshis to two of your addresses. You will have two new currencies of half of a bitcoin each.

3. Why Bitcoins May Not Be Fungible?

While a bitcoin behaves like a 'coin', it has the properties of a ledger. Each transaction refers to its previous transaction, forming a *transaction chain*. Imagine holding a bitcoin that had UTXOs spent in a cybercrime transaction previously. Since people can see this, they may refuse to accept this coin. For this reason, bitcoins may not be always fungible. bitcoins might not be fungible. It lacks the total anonymity of a physical coin.

4. What Does It Mean to Own Bitcoins?

Owning a bitcoin means proving that the previous owner has sent it to your address. It is like proving the ownership of a second-hand car. How would you prove you own the vehicle and haven't stolen it? You must show evidence that the last owner has transferred it to your name. The bitcoin script—ScriptPubKey—does the same. It proves that a UTXO of a previous transaction is sent to your address by providing the public key for verification. However, the previous owner must have acquired the bitcoins legitimately and should not have double-spent them on you.

5. What Does It Mean to Spend Bitcoins?

To spend bitcoins, you must be able to prove that you own them and have approved their spending with your digital signature. The bitcoin script uses your public key and digital signature to prove the same.

6. What Does It Mean to Lose Bitcoins?

You can lose bitcoins either by losing the private key or by sending them to the wrong address. You cannot spend bitcoins if you have lost your private key. Anyone who has access to your private keys can spend your bitcoin. Also, bitcoin transactions are irreversible. You can lose bitcoins if you have sent them to an unknown address by mistake.

7. How to Kill a Bitcoin?

It is possible to transfer bitcoins to an unspendable address, also known as a dead wallet. The bitcoins which are sent to such an address are forever gone. We can't use them again. The procedure is simple; in the transaction output, provide PkScript: OP_RETURN.

8. Is It Possible to Create a Bitcoin Which Anyone Can Spend?

It is possible to create a UTXO which anyone can spend just like anyone who holds a physical coin can spend it. You can do this by constructing a script like below.

> **PkScript:** Empty (it means you are keeping the address of the recipient empty. This is like writing a blank check; whoever holds it can spend it.)
> **SigScript:** OP_TRUE (It is to ensure that the script will do its job despite the information about the recipient is not provided.)

9. What Are Bitcoin Wallets and What Is Their Role?

From constructing a transaction to authenticating it, your bitcoin wallet software will do it in seconds. Some of you who are already into cryptocurrencies must have seen the wallet showing a BTC balance. Now, you know that it is not an account balance. Your wallet keeps track of all the UTXOs you own in various addresses. You can have hundreds of addresses. It is advisable to use a different address each time you receive a change. This makes it challenging to track your real-world identity.

10. Where Do Bitcoins Live?

UTXOs are stored in a unique blockchain database, not in your wallet. Hence, if anyone asks you where bitcoins live, you can answer confidently: They live in the bitcoin blockchain.

11. How Long Does It Take to Send a Bitcoin?

A transaction is confirmed whenever it is included in a valid block. A valid block is created every 10 minutes. Therefore, it can take 10 minutes for a transaction to be completed *with one confirmation*. However, it can vary wildly because of network congestion, hash rate and transaction fees.

12. How Can You Speed Up Your Transaction?

You can add more transaction fees so that miners will be lured to include your transaction in their next block. Also, you may use the off-peak periods when transactions are less. Miners will be more likely to include your transaction even if it has less fees. You can check the off-peak periods on blockchain.com.[1] If the mempool is bigger, it means that there are a lot of pending transactions, and you will have a tough time getting your transaction into a valid block. You should find periods when the mempool size is less. These periods may correspond to night time in the USA when people are sleeping. You can use these periods to send your bitcoins faster and with fewer fees.

1 https://www.blockchain.com/charts/mempool-growth

13. How Many Confirmations are Needed for a Bitcoin Transaction?

If you are sending or receiving high amounts, wait for six confirmations. If you use exchanges to send, receive, buy or sell bitcoins, it will depend on the norms fixed by respective exchanges. For example, in Binance, you will need only one confirmation for deposits, while two confirmations are required for bitcoin withdrawals. Coinbase will require three block confirmations for all kinds of transactions.

Note: Binance and Coinbase are some of the largest crypto exchanges.

14. How to Check if Your Transaction Is Completed?

If you use the wallets provided by exchanges, you will be notified automatically. Else you can use any blockchain explorer to find out. For example, you can use the explorer provided by blockchain.com.[2] Just search the transaction hash in the search field, and it will show you the status of confirmations.

15. Why Is Bitcoin So Slow Compared to Credit Card Payments?

When you pay through a credit card, the credit card company guarantees the seller that the amount will be paid. Money doesn't change hands until the credit card company pays the seller. This settlement period is usually a few days. In the case of bitcoin, the money *moves* to the other person in minutes to hours. However, despite this, credit cards are faster in getting things done. Imagine paying for a T-shirt and there is a long queue behind you. And the seller agrees to accept payment only after three confirmations. That would take a minimum of 30 minutes. Will the people behind you let you stand there for 30 minutes? I don't think so. Instead, you will be forced to pay by credit card or cash. Transaction speed is one of the issues the bitcoin network has been

2 https://www.blockchain.com/explorer

trying to solve for a long time. As we will discuss later, there is a bitcoin fork called Bitcoin Cash which was created precisely for this reason.

REAL EXAMPLES

Example 1: First Bitcoins

In the picture below, you are seeing the bitcoin's first transaction. It is a coinbase transaction created by mining the first block of bitcoin. It was done on 3 January 2009 by Satoshi Nakamoto. This transaction has 0 inputs and 50 BTC outputs.

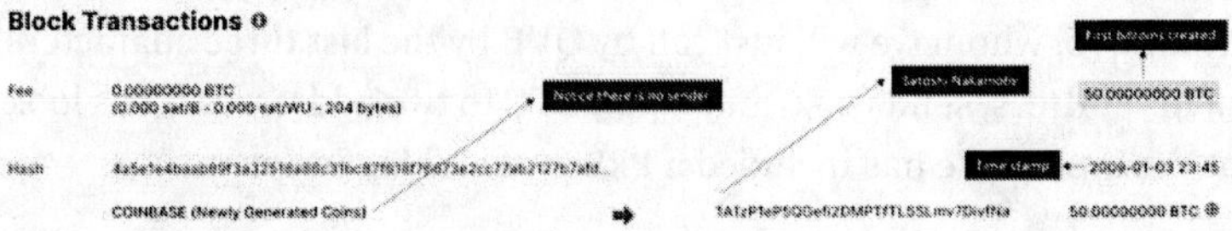

Source: https://www.blockchain.com/btc/tx/4a5e1e4baab89f3a32518a88c31bc87f618f76673e2cc77ab2127b7afdeda33b

Inputs and Outputs of Bitcoins' First Transaction

Notice that the coinbase transaction doesn't have a PkScript in its input because it was not received from anyone.

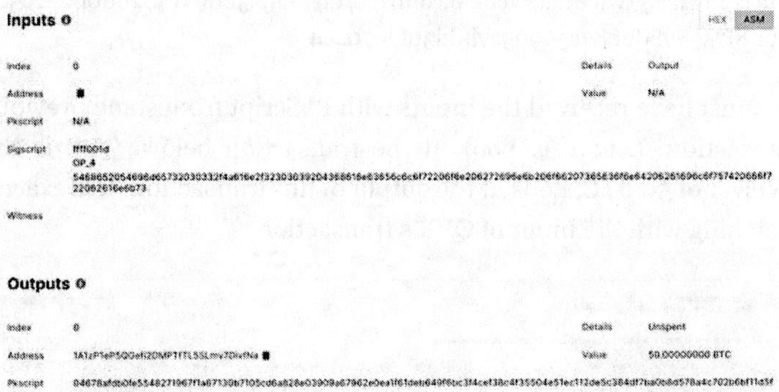

Source: https://www.blockchain.com/btc/tx/4a5e1e4baab89f3a32518a88c31bc87f618f76673e2cc77ab2127b7afdeda33b

Example 2: Let's Look at a Spent Transaction. I found this transaction in Block No. 100000.

Source: https://www.blockchain.com/btc/tx/fff2525b8931402dd09222c50775608f75787bd2b87e56995a7bdd30f79702c4

In this transaction, sender address: 1BnwxHGaFbeUBitpjy2AsKpJ29Ybxntqvb, whom we will just call by QVB by the last three characters of his address, sends 5.56 and 44.44 BTC to two addresses. Let's look at the inputs. He has included a PkScript and SigScript.

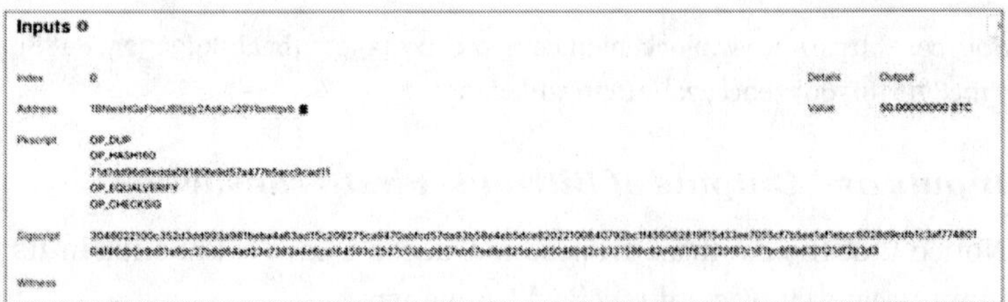

Source: https://www.blockchain.com/btc/tx/fff2525b8931402dd09222c50775608f75787bd2b87e56995a7bdd30f79702c4

He must have received the inputs with PkScript from some previous transaction. Let's see. Look at the transaction below. QVB is the receiver of 50 BTC. Look at the output of this transaction. It is exactly matching with the input of QVB's transaction.

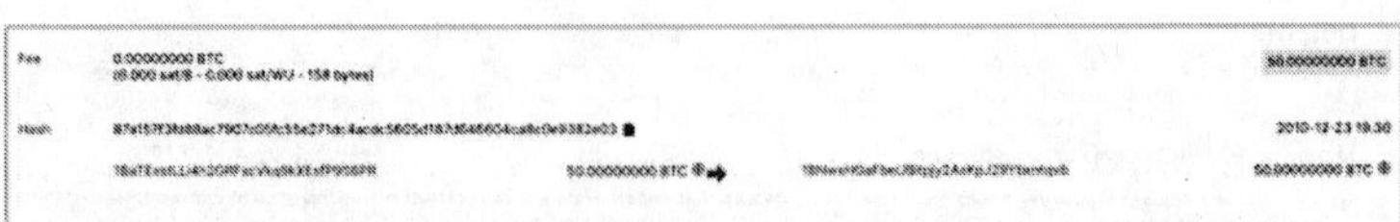

Source: https://www.blockchain.com/btc/tx/87a157f3fd88ac7907c05fc55e271dc4acdc5605d187d646604ca8c0e9382e03

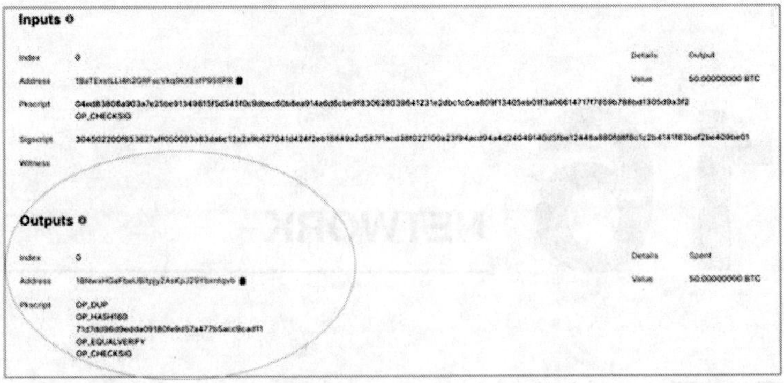

Source: https://www.blockchain.com/btc/tx/87a157f3fd88ac7907c05fc55e271dc4acdc5605d187d646604ca8c0e9382e03

16 NETWORK

Many of us might have seen pictures of the Internet as a globe covered with lightning lines or a cloud. However, the Internet is nothing but a network of billions of computers sending and receiving data through phone cables. In simple words, it is just a bunch of computers talking over the wires.

A website, a Facebook page or a YouTube video doesn't exist on the Internet. It exists in a computer somewhere in the world, accessed via the Internet. For example, whenever you store data in Google Drive, watch a video on YouTube or purchase something from Amazon, your mobile or PC requests these companies' servers to send data. A server is a computer that provides resources, data, services or programs to other computers known as clients. These types of networks are called client-server networks.

The Internet was designed to enable a censorship-free exchange of information. However, with time, the Internet became more and more centralized. By centralized, I mean the computing resources, such as storage and processing power, now lie with a few tech giants such as Google and Amazon. These companies own massive data centres with thousands of powerful servers.

In the following figure, you can see the architecture of the Internet with its different layers. The Internet *layer is a set of protocols or rules* which are abided by computers when sending data. It consists of Internet protocol (IP) and transmission control protocol (TCP). These protocols act as the language which all the network computers understand. Users use web browsers to search the content available in websites hosted in different servers across the world. All the websites follow HTTP. When we connect with any of these websites, our mobile or PC uses TCP port 80. TCP ports are like real-world ports where data is sent and received.

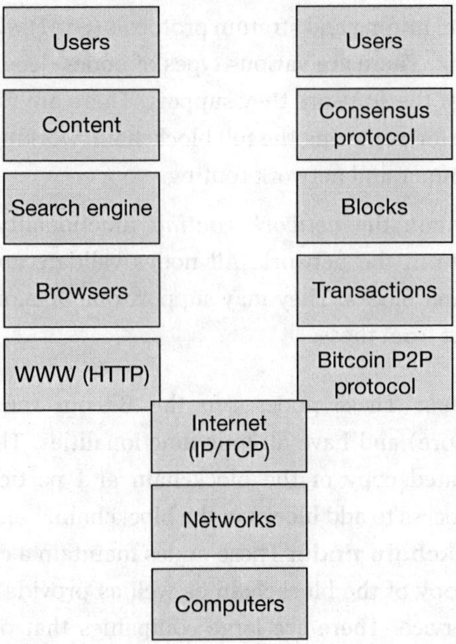

The bitcoin P2P protocol is not a layer above HTTP. It is a layer just above the Internet layer (IP/TCP). Therefore, it is not a website and is not hosted on a server owned by any company or group. It uses TCP port 8333. Each node or computer has the equal right to participate in sending, receiving, validating, maintaining and creating bitcoins. There is no central server, no hierarchy, so we call it a P2P network.

NODES IN THE P2P NETWORK

Nodes are the computers in the bitcoin network that run bitcoin protocol or software. The main bitcoin network consists of around 7,000 to 10,000 nodes which run various versions of Bitcoin Core software (designed by Satoshi and revised by the network many times). In contrast, some run software such as BitcoinJ and Libbitcoin. All these software help in executing the bitcoin protocol. The *extended* bitcoin network includes nodes which implement specialized pool mining and stratum protocols (STM) which are used for pool mining. There are various types of nodes depending on the functionality of the software they support. There are four functions a node can perform: storing the full blockchain, working as a wallet, working as a miner and network routing.

All nodes contain the *network routing* functionality to connect and participate in the network. All nodes validate and propagate transactions and blocks. They may support one or more additional functions apart from these.

Full nodes: These nodes run the Bitcoin reference client (Bitcoin Core) and have all four functionalities. They store the most updated copy of the blockchain and participate in the mining process to add blocks in the blockchain.

Full blockchain node: These nodes maintain a complete and updated copy of the blockchain as well as provide the network routing service. There are large companies that operate these kinds of nodes to enable services such as exchanges, wallets, block explorers and merchant payment processing.

Light nodes: These nodes only maintain an abbreviated copy of the blockchain and verify transactions using a method called 'simplified payment verification' or SPV. These nodes can also participate in mining.

Lightweight wallets: These nodes act as user wallets. These follow SPV for transaction verification and participate in the network through the networking function. These don't take part in mining and don't save full blockchain.

Mining nodes: These nodes participate in the mining process and may or may not store a blockchain. The nodes which mine on their own are called 'solo miners'. Some nodes join a mining pool through STM and don't maintain a blockchain. These are called 'pool miners', and these depend on the blockchain stored in the pool server.

Apart from the above nodes, some nodes act as a gateway server which connects the *nodes running P2P protocol* to the *nodes running other protocols* such as stratum or pool mining protocols. We call these pool protocol 'server nodes'. There are also a few nodes which contain only a wallet and stratum network protocol. These are referred to as 'stratum SPV wallet nodes'.

HOW TO JOIN THE BITCOIN NETWORK?

Your device must be running any of the above nodes to join the bitcoin network. The most common way to join the bitcoin network is by downloading and running a user wallet. When a node is installed and activated, it must establish a connection with at least one peer. There are some long-standing stable nodes in bitcoin called seed nodes. These are in no way special except for being there in the network for long. A new node can connect with one of the seed nodes and ask for the addresses of other nodes. The seed node then responds with the list of addresses. The new node disconnects from the seed node and connects with the peer nodes provided by the seed node. It gets an updated copy of blockchain from its peers.

While making the connections, the new node shares its IP address with its peers. The peers then tell the IP address of the new node to their peers and request them to send their IP address to the new node. A node must relate to a handful of different peers because nodes join and leave the network. If it is rebooted, it remembers the recent list of peers and quickly connects with them. If one of its peers is rebooted, it helps the rebooted node by telling its neighbours to join.

The P2P network is one of the most critical elements in the Bitcoin ecosystem. It is highly secure compared to the client-server technology followed by banks and financial institutions. It is resilient to the single point of failures, hacks, downtimes, fraud and manipulation.

17 BITCOIN BLOCKCHAIN

We have covered various aspects of blockchain in Chapter 13. We will have short discussion on the bitcoin blockchain in this chapter.

BITCOIN BLOCK STRUCTURE

This is the basic structure of a bitcoin block. There are mainly three parts: list of transactions, block header and block identifier.

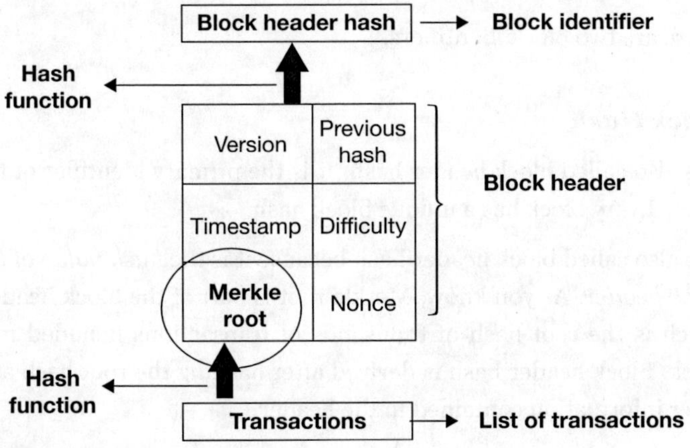

Transactions

- Each transaction in the block is *digitally signed by the owner*.
- There can be thousands of transactions recorded in a block.

- Each of these transactions is hashed.
- Hashes of all the transactions are combined and hashed again to arrive at a single root hash. This root hash is called 'Merkle root'.

Components of Block Header

- **Version:** Blockchain is software. The version of the software is included in the header.
- **Previous block hash:** It links the current block with its last block.
- **Timestamp:** It is the date and time when the block is created. All blocks are chronologically ordered based on timestamps.
- **Merkle root:** It is the root hash of all the transactions in the block.
- **Nonce:** It is an abbreviation for 'number at once'.
- **Difficulty:** It is the complex level of the puzzle.

Block Identifier

There are two block identifiers.

Block Hash

It is also called block header hash. It is the primary identifier of the block. Every block has a unique block hash.

It is also called block header hash because it is the *hash value of the block header*. As you know, Merkle root is part of the block header, which is the root hash of thousands of transactions included in a block. Block header hash is derived after hashing the root hash and other information contained in the header.

- The block header hash is calculated in bitcoin blockchain by running the block header through the SHA 256 hash algorithm *twice*. A different hashing method can be followed for a separate blockchain.

- The block header hash is *not part* of the block structure. It is not sent through the network. Every node or peer computer calculates the block header hash *as part of the verification process* from the information contained in the block header.

Block Height

Imagine a blockchain where each subsequent block is stacked above the previous block forming a vertical chain. Block height of the first block or genesis block is 0. Block height of any block is its position above the genesis block. For example, if a block is positioned above 500,000 blocks from the genesis block, its block height is 500,000. Suppose a new block is added after that, then the new block height will be 500,501. Block height doesn't uniquely identify the block. Two or more blocks can have the same height.

MERKLE ROOT

One of the most critical pieces of information in the block header is the Merkle root. It is derived from the hashes of all transactions included in a block, ensuring that none can be modified without modifying the block hash.

Let's assume that there are four transactions: T1, T2, T3 and T4 (refer to the picture below).

Following is the process of deriving the Merkle root:

1. Hash all four transactions. You will get Hash1, Hash 2, Hash 3 and Hash 4.
2. Concatenate (join) Hash 1 and Hash 2 and run the hash function to derive Hash 12.
3. Concatenate Hash 3 and Hash 4 and run the hash function to derive Hash 34.
4. Concatenate Hash 12 and Hash 34 and run hash function to arrive at Merkle root.

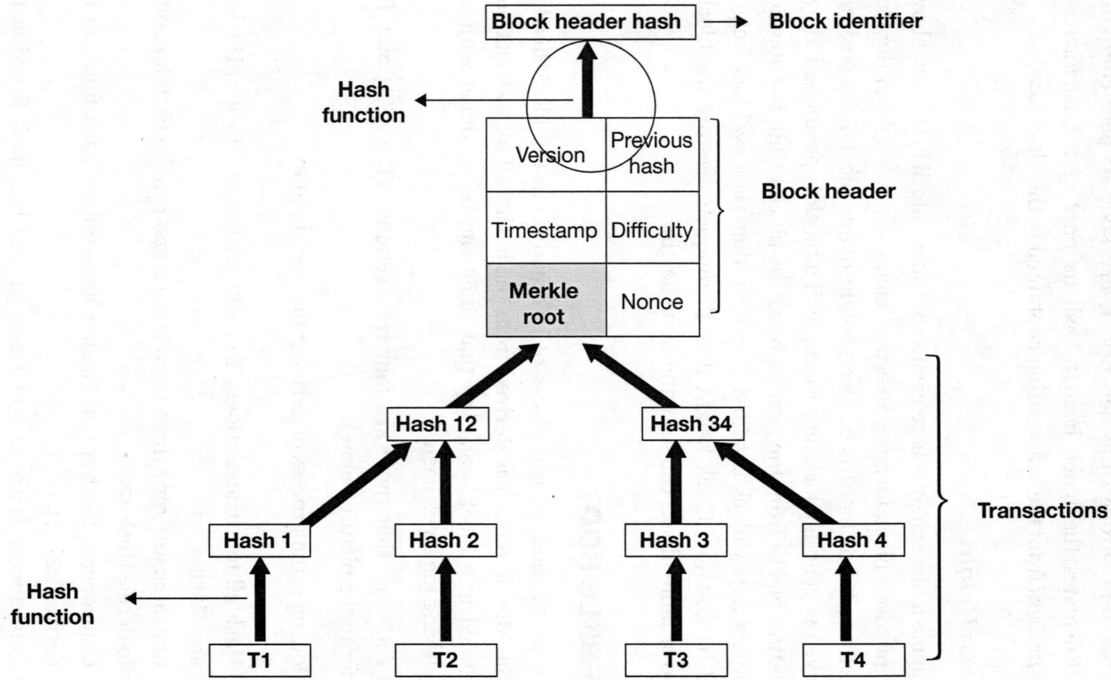

Block header hash
Block identifier
Hash function
Version
Previous hash
Timestamp
Difficulty
Merkle root
Nonce
Block header
Hash 12
Hash 34
Hash 1
Hash 2
Hash 3
Hash 4
Transactions
Hash function
T1
T2
T3
T4

Concept notes:

1. Transaction hashes are also called transaction IDs. For example, the transaction ID for T1 is Hash 1.
2. Markle hash structure resembles a tree. Hence, it is referred to as the Markle tree. It is also called a *binary hash tree* because it always groups all the transaction IDs in pairs. If there happens to be an odd number of transaction IDs, then the last transaction ID is copied and paired with itself.

Benefits of Merkle Root

Let's see some of the benefits of using the Markle root in blockchain.

A single block in blockchain may contain thousands of transactions: Each transaction hash takes up a space of 64 characters or 32 bytes. Processing and verifying all these transaction IDs will require substantial time and processing power. With the help of Markle root, the integrity of all the transactions can be verified easily as you need to check the Markle root, which is only 64 characters.

Even if a single transaction is modified, the block header hash will change: It is tedious to notice tampering when there are a lot of transactions. This problem is solved by including the Markle hash in the block header. Any change in transactions will change the Markle root, further changing the block header hash.

HASH POINTER

If you want to trace tampering in blockchain, you need to go back from the latest block to the tampered block. Hence, a backward-pointing hash arrow provides a good visualization of how to go back and locate modifications. This is called a hash pointer.

Whenever a new block is created, the *previous block hash* is included in the new block header. Previous hash works as a connector between

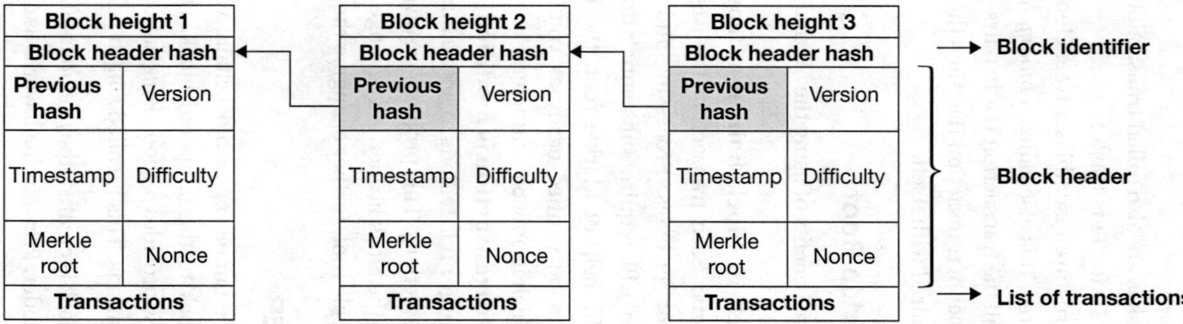

Block height 1
Block header hash
Previous hash
Version
Timestamp
Difficulty
Merkle root
Nonce
Transactions
Block height 2
Block header hash
Previous hash
Version
Timestamp
Difficulty
Merkle root
Nonce
Transactions
Block height 3
Block header hash
Previous hash
Version
Timestamp
Difficulty
Merkle root
Nonce
Transactions
Block identifier
Block header
List of transactions

the last block and the current block. It points to the last block header and its hash. With the hash pointer, we can retrieve information from the previous block header (as you know that block header contains all the information of the block). Further, we can check that the information is not modified (by recalculating the header hash of the previous block and matching with the previous hash included in the current block).

Nonce and difficulty in the block structure play a significant role in deriving the block header hash. The process of deriving block hash is called 'mining'. A valid new block is created at the end of the mining process.

18 HOW DOES IT WORK?

Let's take one simple example: Bob wants to send 10 bitcoins to Murphy.

Let's look at the steps involved.

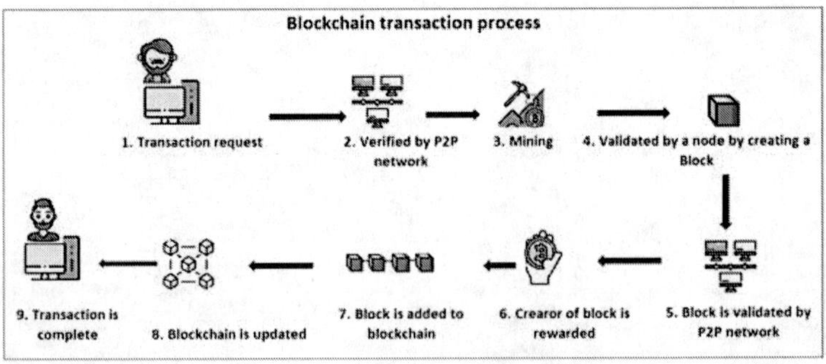

BOB WILL INITIATE THE TRANSACTION

Bob's wallet will construct a bitcoin transaction by accumulating 10 BTC (UTXOs) from various addresses owned by him. It will add Murphy's bitcoin address as the destination address and sign the transaction using Bob's private key. Once he clicks on send, it broadcasts the signed transaction to the neighbouring nodes. These nodes can be wallets, mining nodes, nodes belonging to exchanges or merchants or operated by people doing e-commerce or someone running a node just for fun.

TRANSACTION IS VERIFIED BY THE P2P NETWORK

Once the nodes receive Bob's transaction, they will carry out a validation process. They will check the following:

1. Whether Bob has approved the transaction by signing it digitally. If not, it is a false transaction, and nodes will reject it.
2. Whether he owns 10 BTC involved in the transaction. If not, he doesn't have enough money to spend, and nodes will reject it.
3. Whether this transaction is already included in blockchain. If it is already included, then this new transaction is invalid, as it will result in double-spending. Therefore, nodes will reject it.

Apart from the above checkpoints, there are various other criteria the transaction must satisfy. It must not have an unusual script, size of the transaction should be within the limit, it should have minimum fees, etc. If the transaction is authentic and valid, the nodes will relay the transaction to their neighbouring nodes. Those nodes will validate the transaction and send it to their peers. In this way, the transaction will be flooded or propagated through the whole network, and every node will have a chance to validate them.

MINING

- All the nodes which have validated the transaction store the transaction in the pool of unconfirmed transactions called 'mempool'. It is important to note that there is no single mempool. There is a mempool in every node. The transaction set contained in the mempool of nodes may be different because of the timing of transaction propagation. Different nodes will receive transactions at different times due to the small amount of time lag in the network. Even if the ordering of transactions is different, 99 per cent of transactions will probably overlap in all the mempools.

- Eventually, Bob's transaction will be picked up by the mining nodes. This is what miners (or mining nodes) will do:
    - They will construct a candidate block with a block header consisting of a link to the previous block hash to establish its position in blockchain, a timestamp and a few other details. It will have at least one transaction, that is, the coinbase transaction, which will reward the miners with new bitcoins if they can validate the block.
    - They will send this block to their mining equipment and start looking for transactions to add. The mining equipment competes with other mining nodes to solve the POW puzzle.
    - They will check their mempools and include the unconfirmed transactions in the candidate block. Bitcoin block size is limited to 1 MB, containing anywhere between 1,000 and 2,500 transactions. Since the space is limited, transactions that pay *more fees per byte* are included with priority. The intention is to maximize the profit per transaction. Fees often spike at times of network congestion resulting from high transaction volume. For example, in April 2021, average transaction fees reached $59. Let's say Bob has included enough fees, and mining nodes have included his transaction in their candidate block.

As they add transactions, the block gets filled, and whenever they add some transactions, they will send it to the mining equipment. The mining equipment continues to solve the POW.

CREATING A VALID BLOCK

The miner who is lucky enough to solve the POW puzzle first converts their candidate block into a valid block. Then it sends the valid block to its neighing peers.

VALIDATING THE BLOCK

The block is then propagated through the network the same way transactions are propagated. Hence, both transactions and blocks are flooded through the network at any point in time. Once the block reaches other miners, they validate it quickly, and if it is valid, they abandon working on it and start working on a new block. All nodes in the network validate the block and take the transaction out of their mempool, which is confirmed now. Solving the POW puzzle is difficult, but validating it is easy and takes a few seconds, even if there is a long list of checks to be done. Below are some of the critical checkpoints.

- Block size is valid.
- Transactions are valid.
- The new block contains the previous block hash.
- The new block is part of the 'longest chain'.

REWARDING THE MINER

The miner who solved the POW is rewarded with new bitcoins through the coinbase transaction. However, they would receive this reward after 100 confirmations.

ADDING THE BLOCK TO THE BLOCKCHAIN

Every node that has verified the new block's validity adds the block to its blockchain.

UPDATING THE BLOCKCHAIN

Eventually, all the network nodes check the validity of the new block and add it to their blockchain.

TRANSACTION IS COMPLETED

Bob's transaction is completed once it is added to a valid block. At this point, it is said to have been completed with one confirmation.

Once one more block is added, it will have two confirmations. As we will see in the next chapter, a valid new block may get replaced by another valid block. Therefore, it is suggested to wait for two–three confirmations. And if you are sending a large amount, you should wait for at least six confirmations. Bitcoin blocks are created on average of 10 minutes; hence, that is 60 minutes of waiting time. However, it is worth waiting if you are sending $100 million in BTC. It is almost impossible to redo the POW and replace 6 blocks in less than 10 minutes.

There is no final conformity of transactions in bitcoin. it is theoretically possible to reverse all the transactions if some computer can redo the POW for all the blocks (700,000 plus until now) within the time next block is created. It is practically impossible with present-day technology.

Coming to our example, once Murphy's wallet receives the block containing Bob's transaction, he will know that the transaction has been confirmed.

19 MINING BITCOINS

Mining is one of the most esoteric aspects of bitcoin for anyone who is entering the crypto world. However, it is nothing but the process of recording transactions in the blockchain. Since everyone has a copy of the blockchain, it is crucial that everyone records valid transactions and maintains an identical copy of the correct blockchain. Ensuring that everyone behaves honestly and has a replica of the accurate ledger is called the problem of decentralized consensus. We have discussed the conceptual underpinning of mining in Chapter 9. Here I will answer everything concerning bitcoin mining. All the questions are answered in a logical sequence.

TWENTY-ONE MINING QUESTIONS ANSWERED!

1. Why Does Anyone Choose to Become a Miner?

It is to make a profit by earning new bitcoins and collecting transaction fees (called block reward).

2. How Do Miners Reach a Consensus about the State of a Ledger?

The ledger copy available with each node should have the same order of transactions. Else, there will be many different versions of the blockchain. The aim of having a synchronized distributed true ledger will fail. Let's elaborate this through an example.

Transaction A: Bob has transferred 100 BTC to Murphy. This transaction is broadcasted at 12.00 PM.

Transaction B: Murphy has transferred 50 BTC to Lindy. This transaction is broadcasted at 12.05 PM.

Both transactions A and B will be broadcasted to the P2P network. This network can have thousands of participants spread throughout the world. They must own an identical copy of ledger. The circles in the below picture represent nodes. Dark nodes received transaction A first and then transaction B and updated their books accordingly. At the same time, the white nodes received transaction B first and then transaction A. They have updated their books accordingly.

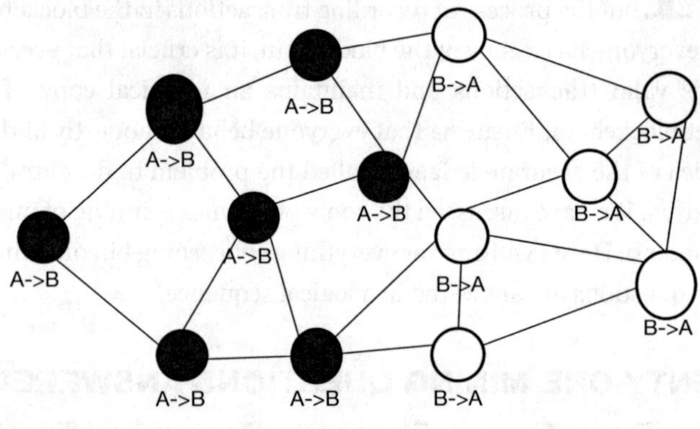

Ledger of Dark Nodes

Time	Transaction
12.02 PM	Transaction A: Bob sent $100 to Murphy.
12.07 PM	Transaction B: Murphy sent $50 to Lindy.

Ledger of White Nodes

Time	Transaction
12.06 PM	Transaction B: Murphy sent $50 to Lindy.
12.07 PM	Transaction A: Bob sent $100 to Murphy.

The problem is that books of dark and white nodes do not match as they have different orders of transactions. White nodes will reject transaction B because, as per them, Murphy is trying to spend 50 BTC he doesn't have. But he owns 50 BTC sent by Bob. Since dark nodes got the order of transactions correct, their book reflects ledger's true state where Murphy owned 50 BTC and sent 50 BTC. The ledger of white nodes is incorrect, but it is not their fault. They received the transactions in a different order. It takes time for transactions to propagate through the whole network. Some nodes will receive some transactions earlier than others. This can happen due to many factors such as connectivity, Internet speed, servers, geographical distance and bandwidth. How to ensure that every node gets the correct version of ledger?

The Solution: Blocks

As discussed in Chapter 9, we cannot control the rate at which the transactions are created. But we can control the rate at which they will be recorded in the ledger. Hence, it is better to record transactions in batches or blocks.

Recording transactions in blocks creates two benefits: It slows down the data entry to the ledger. Transactions get more time to reach a maximum number of nodes. Instead of agreeing on the order of transactions, nodes can agree on the order of blocks created less frequently. A block is more likely to reach all the bookkeepers (nodes) in the network before another is created. Transactions are completed block by block. Completed transactions are excluded while creating the next block.

3. How Do Miners Produce New Blocks?

For example, below is a blockchain. There are three blocks. The fourth block needs to be created.

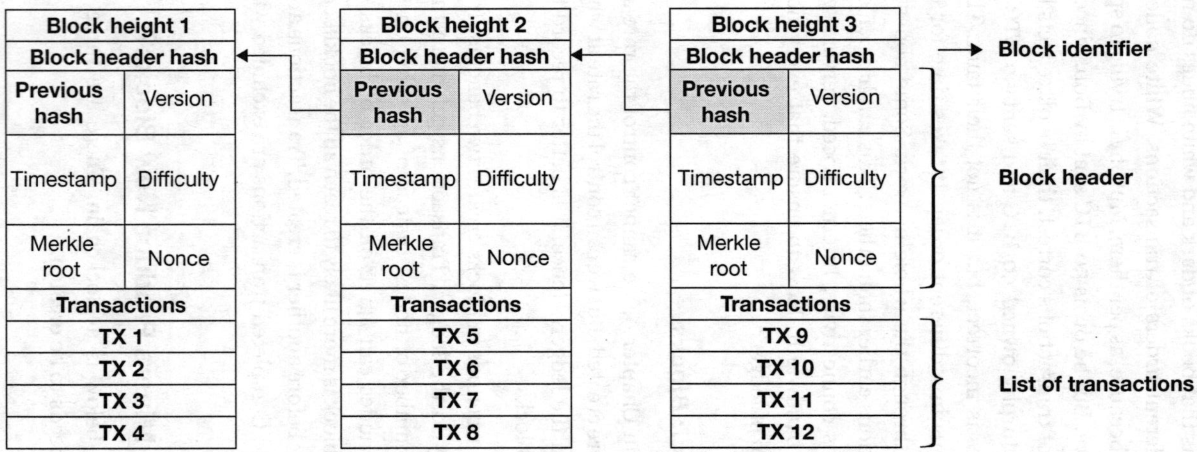
Block height 1
Block header hash
Previous hash
Version
Timestamp
Difficulty
Merkle root
Nonce
Transactions
TX 1
TX 2
TX 3
TX 4
Block height 2
Block header hash
Previous hash
Version
Timestamp
Difficulty
Merkle root
Nonce
Transactions
TX 5
TX 6
TX 7
TX 8
Block height 3
Block header hash
Previous hash
Version
Timestamp
Difficulty
Merkle root
Nonce
Transactions
TX 9
TX 10
TX 11
TX 12
Block identifier
Block header
List of transactions

Here are the pending transactions.

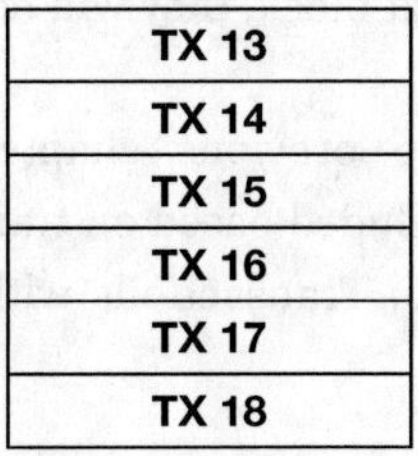

There are four miners. They have collected the pending transactions *in their* mempool, which they have heard, and constructed a candidate block.

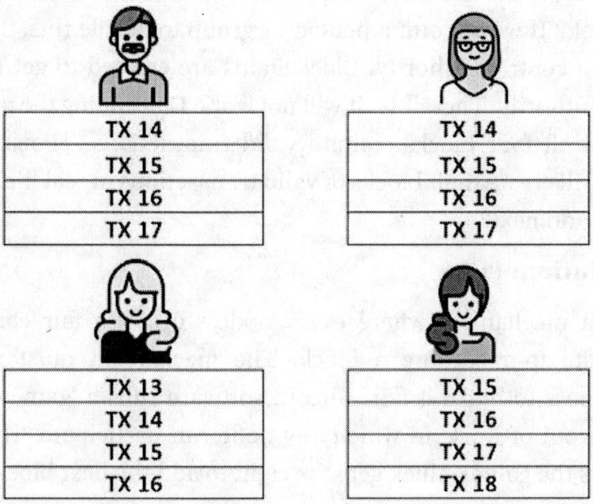

Notes:

1. Different blocks can contain a different set of valid pending transactions.
2. All miners know the chronological order of blocks and the transactions included in those blocks. They can see that three blocks have been completed, and block 3 is the latest.

Transactions 1–12 are already included in these blocks. Hence while creating the next block, they will not consider transactions 1–12.

3. As discussed in the previous chapter, miners choose the transactions to be included based on transaction fees associated with the transactions. Transactions with high transaction fees are prioritized.

4. How to Decide Who Will Get the Right to Add the Next Block?

The problem: In a decentralized network with thousands of nodes, where everyone is anonymous, how can we decide who will create the next block? If we appoint a person or group to decide this, they will become a central authority. Blockchains are created to get rid of a central authority. Therefore, it will not work. Continuing the previous example, all four blocks contain valid transactions. Thousands of miners will create their blocks of valid transactions in real life. Which block to add next?

The solution: POW

Design a mechanism where every node will get a fair chance to participate in recording a block. The mechanism must rely on randomness to make it fair. Bitcoin software runs a 'game of luck' called 'proof of work' in which any node can participate. The node that wins the game of luck gets the right to add the next block.

5. What Is POW, and How Is It Played?

Game of luck: Bitcoin software fixes a target hash for the new block and challenges the miners to generate a block hash smaller than the target hash. The miner who generates a block hash smaller than the target hash wins and gets to create the next block. In other words, their candidate block becomes a valid block. For example, let's say the target hash is 100. Every miner will compete to generate a block hash smaller than 100. If someone generates a hash, for example, 73, they win the game, as this hash is smaller than the target hash.

Do you remember that hash is a special kind of number called hexadecimal number? We use decimal numbers for day-to-day calculations, consisting of nine digits, 0–9. Computers use hexadecimal numbers in certain cases, such as hash. It has six more digits from 10 to 15 represented by A–F. For example, below is a hash. You can see that only letters A–F are used along with digits 0–9. All these are digits.

An example hash is as follows:

5e884898da28047151d0e56f8dc6292773603d0d6aabbdd62a11ef7
21d1542d8

Decimal:	0	1	2	3	4	5	6	7	8	9	10	11	12	13	14	15
Hexadecimal:	0	1	2	3	4	5	6	7	8	9	A	B	C	D	E	F

Imagine that there is a blackboard where all possible hash values are written in descending order from top to bottom. The largest number is written on the top row, and the smallest number is written on the base row. The largest number shall be a string of 64 Fs. The smallest number must be a string of 64 zeroes. All possible hashes would fall between these two rows. Each raw represents a hash value. The largest hashes will be closer to the top row, moderately large ones will be in the middle and the smallest ones will be closer to the base row.

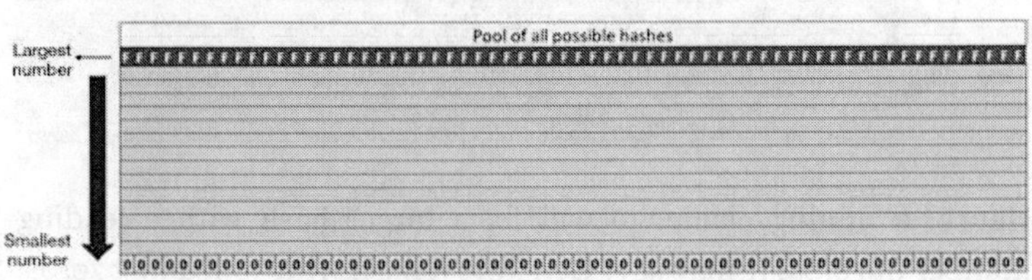

For example, a hash starting with a leading number of Fs will be somewhere on the top of the hash pool.

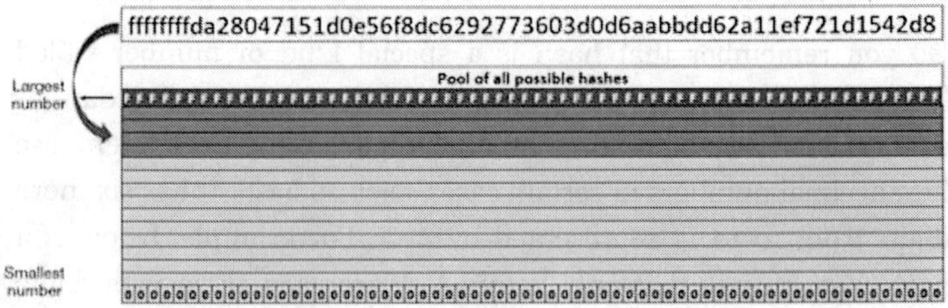

The hash number we have mentioned before will be somewhere in the middle of the hash pool.

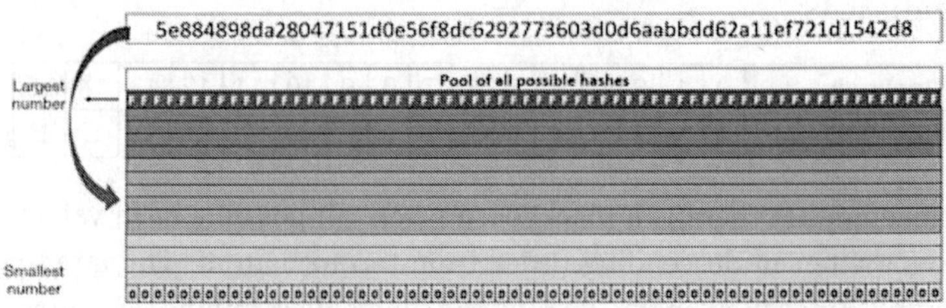

A hash with a 'string of leading zeros' will be somewhere closer to the lowest row of the hash pool.

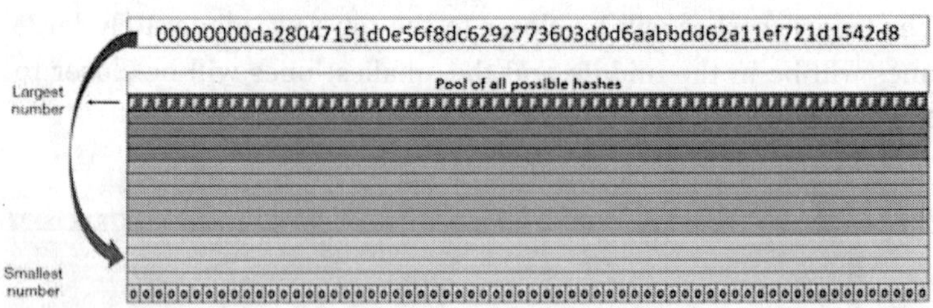

Hence, a mining challenge will fix a target hash with a leading number of zeros. It may say: Generate a hash with 10 leading zeros. The higher the number of zeros at the beginning, the smaller is the number. Look at the below picture. Let's assume that a number with 10 leading zeros exists below the mining threshold line. The mining challenge is to find a number below that line (within the white zone). Once a node finds a hash below that line, it is said to have created a 'valid block hash', and its block is *valid*.

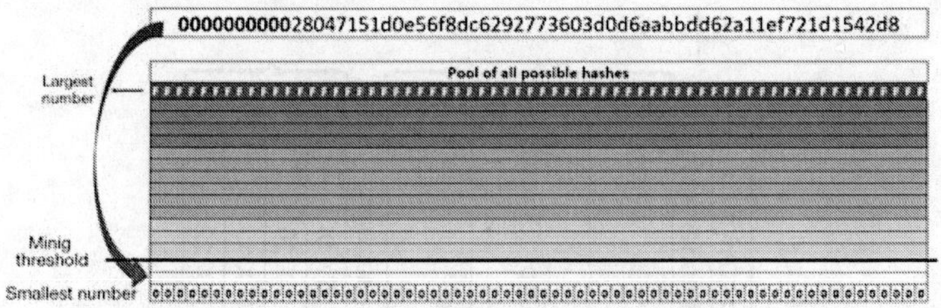

6. What Is the Role of Nonce in POW?

Let's continue with the previous example and see how we can play the game of luck. This is the blockchain we have, and we will create the next block.

Let's assume that the target hash fixed by the blockchain protocol for creating Block 4 is a 'hash with 10 leading zeros'. We need to generate a block hash with 10 leading zeros for Block 4. Below are the pending transactions in our mempool.

TX 13
TX 14
TX 15
TX 16
TX 17
TX 18

Let's collect some of the pending transactions and try to create Block 4. Since the block size is limited to 1 MB, we may not be able to add all the pending transactions we have in the mempool.

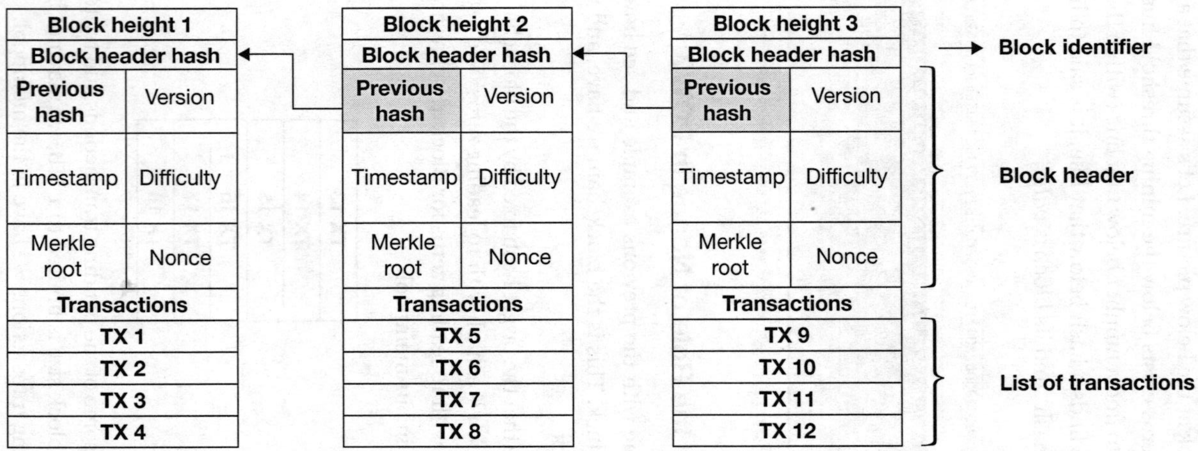

Block height 1
Block header hash
Previous hash
Version
Timestamp
Difficulty
Merkle root
Nonce
Transactions
TX 1
TX 2
TX 3
TX 4
Block height 2
Block header hash
Previous hash
Version
Timestamp
Difficulty
Merkle root
Nonce
Transactions
TX 5
TX 6
TX 7
TX 8
Block height 3
Block header hash
Previous hash
Version
Timestamp
Difficulty
Merkle root
Nonce
Transactions
TX 9
TX 10
TX 11
TX 12
Block identifier
Block header
List of transactions

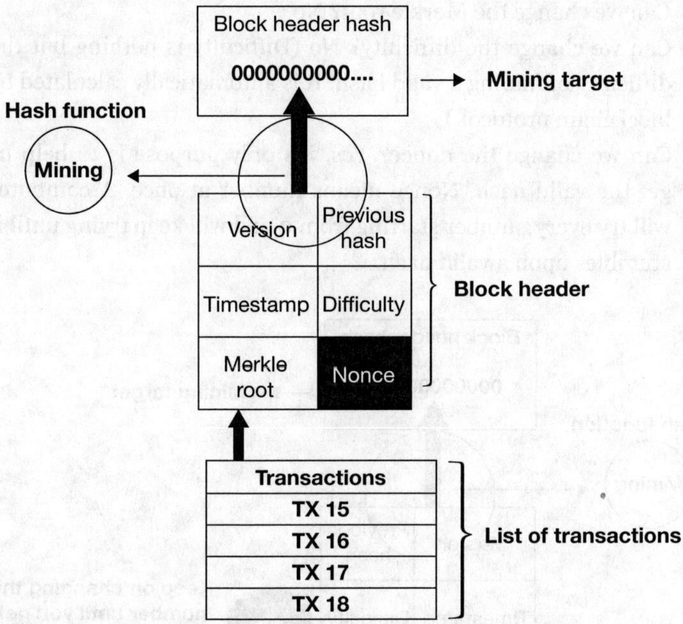

We have collected transactions 15, 16, 17 and 18. Now the only way to generate a hash starting with 10 zeroes is to change the block's content and experiment by running a hash function. Let's see what we can change:

- Can we change the list of transactions included in the block? We can change the combinations of transactions, but we can't change their content. Moreover, there will only be a few thousand transactions to choose from. The chance of getting a valid hash by changing the combinations of transactions is infinitesimal. It will not work.
- Can we change the version? No
- Can we change the previous hash? No
- Can we change the timestamp? No (There is more to it. We will discuss shortly.)

- Can we change the Merkle root? No
- Can we change the difficulty? No (Difficulty is nothing but the difficulty of finding a valid hash. It is automatically calculated by blockchain protocol.)
- Can we change the nonce? *Yes,* it's only purpose is to help us get the valid hash. Nonce means number at once. A computer will try every number starting from 0 and will keep trying until it stumbles upon a valid hash.

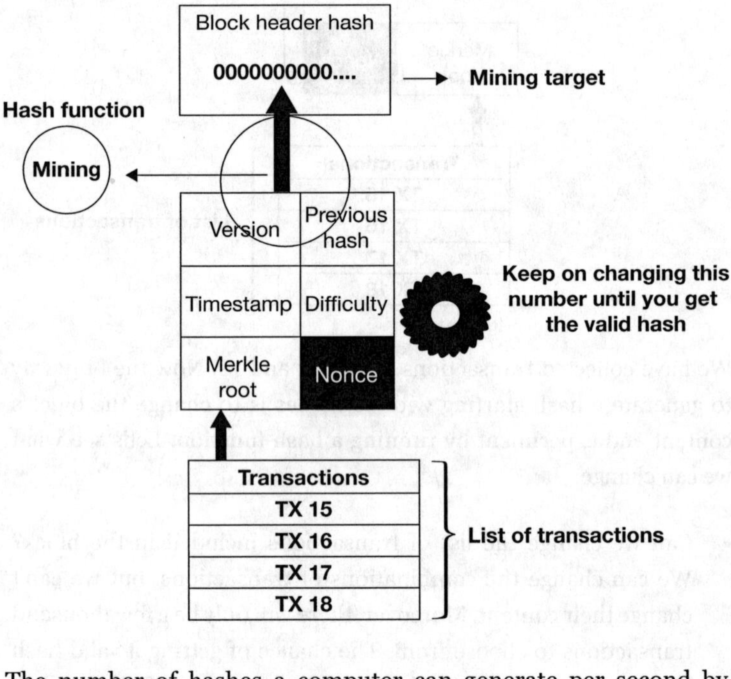

The number of hashes a computer can generate per second by changing the nonce is called the 'hash rate'. Nowadays, special mining devices are available to generate trillions of hashes per second. It is difficult to find a hash with a certain number of leading zeros. More the number of leading zeros, harder it is to find.

7. What Makes POW a Game of Luck?

Suppose for creating Block 4, we started changing nonce from 0 to 1 to 2 ... n. Can you spot something noticeable in the below picture? There is a relationship between change in nonce and change in hash. For example, when the nonce is increased, hash is decreased. We can spot a logical relationship. If we automate this logic in computer software, we will solve all future challenges.

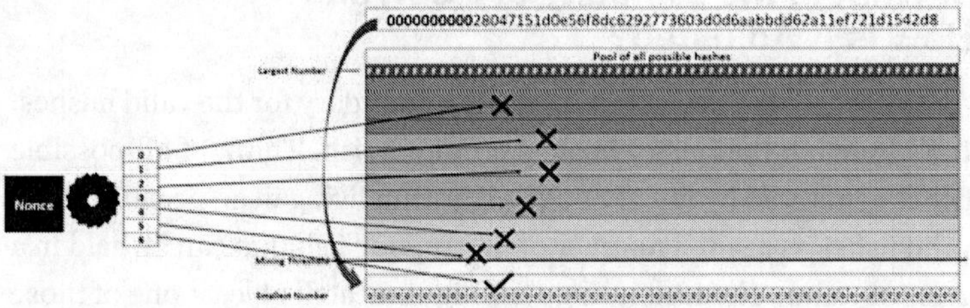

The Problem: If someone can spot *any predictable relationship* between change in nonce to change in hash, they will be able to generate valid blocks by executing a formula. They will gain a substantial advantage over others.

The solution: There is an inbuilt solution in the hash function itself. Yes, it is the avalanche effect. Even an atomic change in data causes a catastrophic change in the hash. It is impossible to find any relationship between the change in data and change in hash. Hence, no one can derive an equation for finding a target hash by relating the nonce changes to the hash changes. Changes in nonce will produce random hashes. Only by chance can one get the target hash. Therefore, it is the avalanche effect of hash that makes POW a game of luck.

In the below illustration, you can see a change in nonce-produced random hashes. You cannot find a shortcut for the solution. Your computer must keep on trying until it gets it by chance. This requires huge computing power and electricity supply.

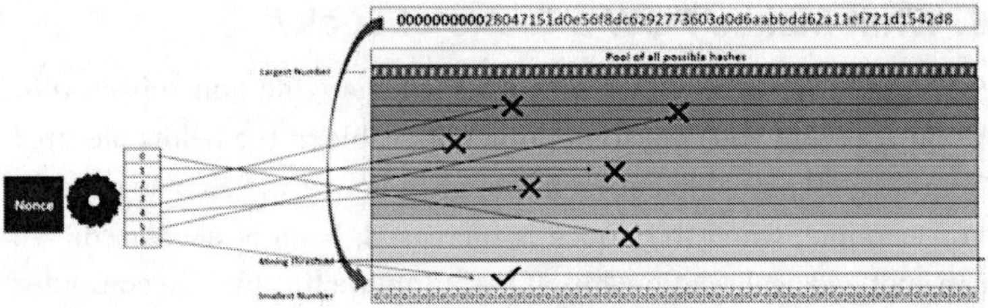

8. What Is the Difficulty of POW, and How Is It Adjusted?

As discussed, the target number sets a boundary for the valid hashes. Let's imagine that every hash is a unique fish. Think of all possible fishes generated by the SHA 256 algorithm living in an ocean and the valid fishes as a small number of tiny unique fish that can be held in a glass of water. The task is to go fishing and catch at least one of those tiny unique fishes from the ocean. If we reduce the glass size, the number of valid fish will reduce, and it will become more and more difficult to catch a valid fish from the ocean.

For example, let's say the hash is a six-digit decimal number. X means that any number from 0 to 9 can take its place.

XXXXXX = It can hold any number between 0 to 999,999. It means that we have 1,000,000 possible hashes.

If the target hash is set to one leading zero,

0XXXXX = The possible hashes will fall within 0–99,999. It means that there will be only 100,000 valid hashes.

If the target hash is set to two leading zeroes,

00XXXX = The possible hashes will fall within 0–9,999. It means that there will be only 10,000 valid hashes.

By observing the above pattern, you can derive a formula: If the hash consists of H number of digits and the target hash consists of N number leading zeros, the number of valid hashes will be 10^{H-N}

For example, our hash is six digits, and suppose the target hash contains four leading zeros, then the number of valid hashes will be $10^{6-4} = 100$

A simple formula can find the chance of finding valid hashes: Number of valid hashes/Total number of hashes = 100/1,000,000 = 0.01 per cent.

You can see how adding leading zeros increases the difficulty and reduces the chance of getting a valid hash.

Let's extend the example to real hashes. As you know, Hash is a 64-digit hexadecimal number. There are 16 digits instead of 10. Therefore, we can modify our formula by replacing 10 with 16.

Hence, for the total number of hashes that is possible:

Let's say the bitcoin protocol requires a target hash of 18 leading zeros. The total number of valid hashes that is possible within this pool is = $16^{64-18} = 16^{46}$

16^{46}	=	24,519,928,653,854,200,000,000,000,000,000,000,000,000,000,000,000,000,000.00000000000000000000
16^{64}	=	115,792,089,237,316,000,000,000,000,000,000,000,000,000,000,000,000,000,000,000,000,000,000,000,000,000.00000000000000000000
	Probbaliity of gerring a valid hash if the target hash starts with 22 zeros	0.0000000000000000002 %

16^{46} is a huge number. But in comparison to 16^{64}, it is an extremely tiny number. 16^{64} is around the number of atoms in our universe.

The probability of finding a valid hash: $16^{46}/16^{64}$ = 0.000000000000 0000002 per cent.

How does this probability make you feel? You may instead win a lottery rather than find a valid hash. If the number of leading zeros in the target hash increases, finding a valid hash becomes more difficult and vice versa.

9. How Is the Mining Difficulty Calculated?

Difficulty = Current target/Maximum target. The maximum target was the target which was fixed when the first block of bitcoin was mined. The current target is the target for the current block. Mining difficulty for initial blocks of bitcoins was 1. Now it is around 25 trillion. It means that it is 25 trillion times more difficult to mine a block now than the initial block.

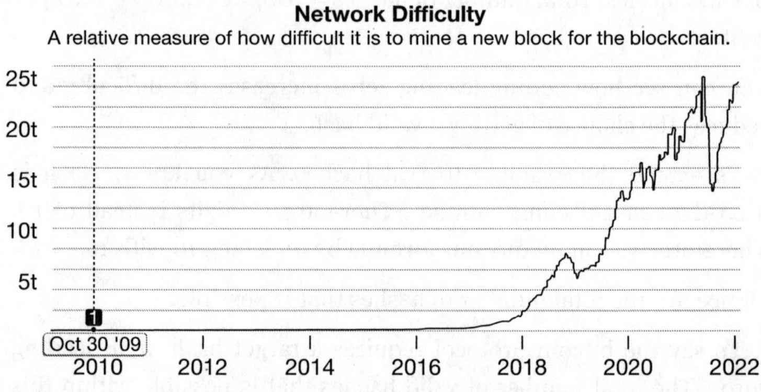

Source: https://www.blockchain.com/charts/difficulty

10. How Is the Mining Difficulty Adjusted?

The bitcoin protocol is designed to produce 1 valid block in 10 minutes. If blocks are produced too fast, it will create a problem in reaching consensus, and if blocks are produced too slow, people will not use them for transactions. You could have used your laptop to mine bitcoins when bitcoin was introduced. But as bitcoin became well known, people worldwide, including corporations, started mining bitcoin. They started using specialized, powerful devices which could create trillions of hashes per second. With this much hash power, a few companies would have mined all the bitcoin long ago. Satoshi might have foreseen this situation; hence, he programmed an inbuilt protection mechanism in the bitcoin software. The more hash power is used to mine the block, the more difficult the target hash level becomes. It means that the number of leading zeros in the target hash will increase.

The difficulty is adjusted automatically after 2016 blocks, roughly 2 weeks considering that 1 block takes around 10 minutes. If the last 2016 blocks took less than 2 weeks to mine, the difficulty is increased, and if they took more than 2 weeks, the difficulty is reduced. This is an elegant solution to keep the issuance of bitcoin consistent. A simple code could handle thousands of miners, organizations with industry-level mining capacity and giant mining pools. No matter how hard you try, it gets harder.

11. What if a Miner Runs Out of Nonces?

Mining nodes try different nonces to generate the block hash. If they are lucky, they will get a block hash below the target hash. However, there is a problem with nonces. They are not infinite. You can't keep incrementing the nonce beyond a limit. There is a cap to the nonces, around 4.2 billion. There is only 32-bit space allocated for nonce within the bitcoin block. A 32-bit number will look like this:

x	x	x	x	x	x	x	x	x	x	x	x	x	x	x	x	x	x	x	x	x	x	x	x	x	x	x	x	x	x	x	x
0/1	0/1	0/1	0/1	0/1	0/1	0/1	0/1	0/1	0/1	0/1	0/1	0/1	0/1	0/1	0/1	0/1	0/1	0/1	0/1	0/1	0/1	0/1	0/1	0/1	0/1	0/1	0/1	0/1	0/1	0/1	0/1

Think of X as memory space. Since computers store data in binary digits, each X can store either a 0 or 1. Therefore, there can be 32 bits of 2 possible values. This means that it can hold 4,294,967,296 possible values. This kind of storage is called unsigned bits, which means that negative numbers are not allowed. Hence, a nonce can be between 0 and 4,294,967,295. Since one nonce can generate one hash, the total number of hashes that a miner can generate is limited to only 4.2 billion.

Let's pick up the example we have discussed under difficulty.

Suppose the target hash starts with 18 leading zeros. It means that we must find a hash from valid hashes. However, remember that the range of all possible hashes is inconceivably gigantic. The probability of randomly picking up a valid hash is 0.00000000000000000002 per cent. And the probability of getting a valid hash within the 4.2 billion hashes generated by all possible nonces = 4.2B × 0.00000000000000000002 per cent = 0.0000000001 per cent.

Since the probability of stumbling upon a valid hash with 4.2 billion nonces is only 0.0000000001 per cent, miners can run out of nonces often. An average miner generates around 100 million hashes per second. 4.2 billion hashes will take only 40 seconds. What will they do after that? They will have to wait until some other miner creates a new block. It is also possible that all the miners fail to get the valid hash in 10 minutes. This would jeopardize the whole Bitcoin system.

How to Solve This Problem?

The solution is provided by the timestamp contained in the block header. As you know, time never stops. Bitcoin uses Unix time as a timestamp. The Unix time or POSIX time or Unix timestamp is the 'number of seconds that have elapsed since 1 January 1970 (midnight UTC/GMT), not counting leap seconds. You can google the current Unix time and find a number like below.

It changes every second. And it changes block hash completely because of the avalanche effect. Hence, before the miner even finishes their arsenal of 4.2 billion nonces, the block information gets updated. They can use the same nonces again because they might not have worked before one second, but they will generate brand new hashes in this second because of a tiny change in the timestamp.

But what if a miner can generate more than 4.2 billion hashes per second? With the advent of application-specific integrated circuit (ASIC) mining, miners can generate terahashes per second. For example, Antminer S19 Pro can generate 100 terahash/second. One terahash is equal to 1,000 billion hashes. It will run out of 4.2 billion nonces within a fraction of a second. Then it will have to wait for the rest of the second to complete so that those 4.2 billion nonces can be used again. This is a sheer waste of capacity.

The network has identified a new source of change within the block header. If you remember, every block contains a coinbase transaction. And a coinbase transaction doesn't need an unlocking script or ScriptSig. It frees up space from 2 to 100 bytes. Except for one instruction on code script execution, block height and hash of miner's address, the rest of the space can be used for 'the extra nonce'. Since the change in coinbase transaction changes the Merkle root and block hash, it is as effective as the original nonce space. Extra nonce takes up 8 bytes or 64 bits of space in coinbase transactions. Thirty-two bits of standard nonce along with 64 bits of extra nonce can generate up to or 79,228,160,000,000,000,0 00,000,000 nonces or hash values. It is way more than the current cumulative hash rate of all the mining devices around the world. And these hashes become brand new after every second.

When writing this book, the whole bitcoin network was generating around 180 million trillion hashes per second. Miners need not worry about running out of nonces for the time being.

Total number of hashes available in hand	79,228,160,000,000,000,000,000,000
Total numer of hashes per second at present	180,000,000,000,000,000,000

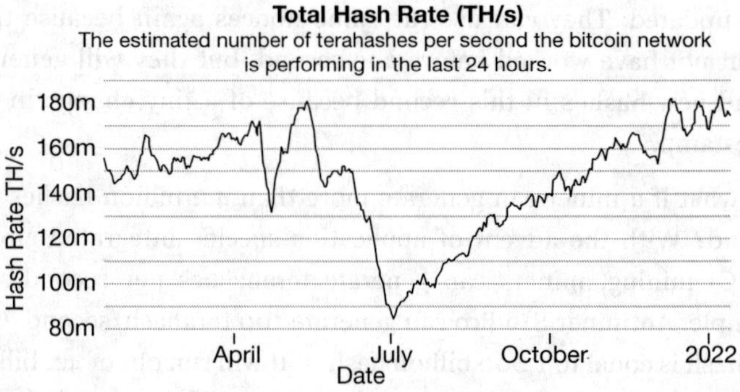

Source: https://www.blockchain.com/charts/hash-rate

12. What Happens after You Create a Valid Block?

If you can mine a valid block, you will send it to your peers for verification. Continuing our previous example, suppose while working on a block, say Block 4, you receive a valid Block 4 from your peers; you will abandon mining Block 4, add it to your blockchain and start working on Block 5. Every node checks the validity of a new block and adds to its copy of the blockchain.

13. What if Two or More Miners Produce a Valid Block Simultaneously?

Let's continue with the previous example. We have three blocks in the blockchain. Miners are trying to create Block 4.

The problem: Suppose both Sam and Lindy have created their *valid blocks* simultaneously. Both the blocks have the right to become Block 4. Whose block shall we choose?

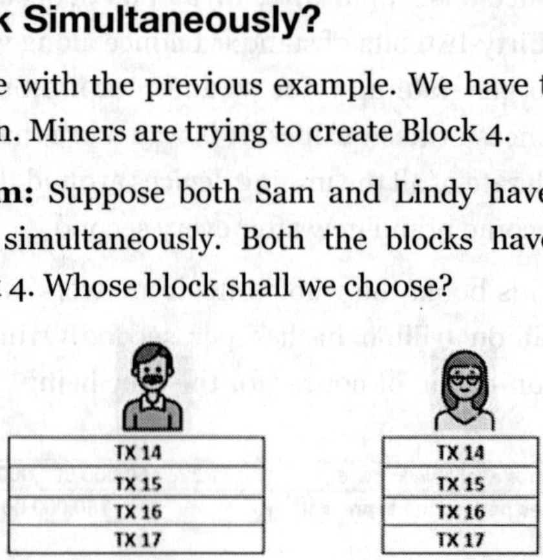

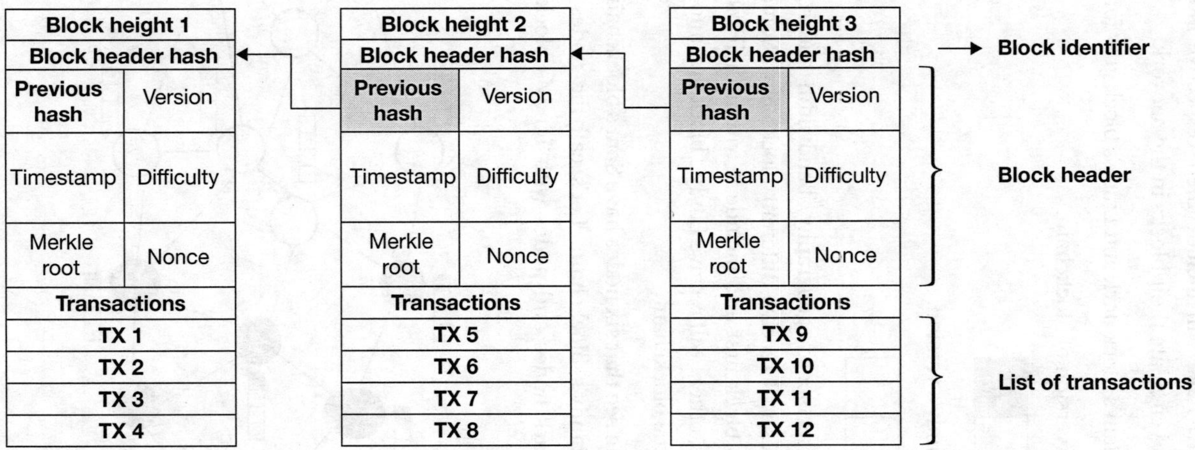

Block height 1
Block header hash
Previous hash
Version
Timestamp
Difficulty
Merkle root
Nonce
Transactions
TX 1
TX 2
TX 3
TX 4
Block height 2
Block header hash
Previous hash
Version
Timestamp
Difficulty
Merkle root
Nonce
Transactions
TX 5
TX 6
TX 7
TX 8
Block height 3
Block header hash
Previous hash
Version
Timestamp
Difficulty
Merkle root
Nonce
Transactions
TX 9
TX 10
TX 11
TX 12
Block identifier
Block header
List of transactions

The solution: Each will include their respective blocks in their blockchain and circulate their blocks in the network.

I have made Sam's block dark and Lindy's block grey for visual ease.

Here is Sam's version of blockchain.

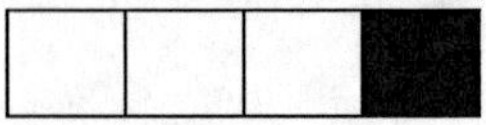

And here is Lindy's version.

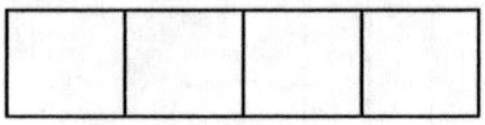

Due to Internet speed, geography, bandwidth and server issues, different nodes will receive different blocks first. Some nodes will receive Sam's block first and include it within their blockchain. At the same time, others will receive Lindy's block first and append it to their copy of the blockchain.

Below, you can see that six nodes have Sam's blockchain, and seven nodes have Lindy's blockchain. Let's call the nodes with Sam's blockchain dark nodes and nodes with Lindy's blockchain white nodes.

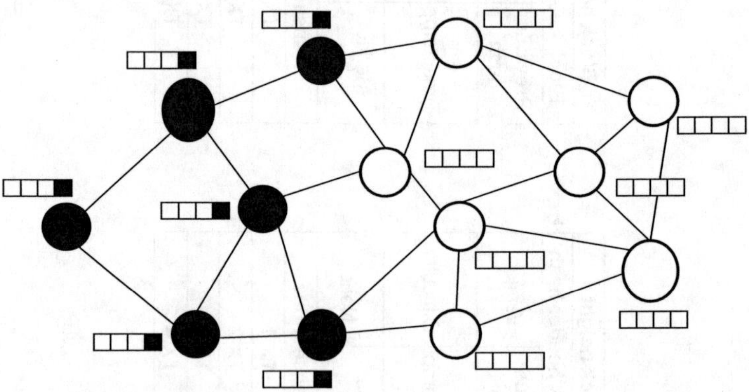

At this point, there are two groups of nodes with four blocks. We cannot say whose blockchain is the final one. Hence, we will wait for the next block to be mined. There is a high probability that one of the white nodes will create the next block. Why? Because they have more nodes, and more nodes mean more hashing power.

Let's say one of the nodes within white nodes has created Block 5. White nodes have the updated blockchain because they have a new valid Block 5.

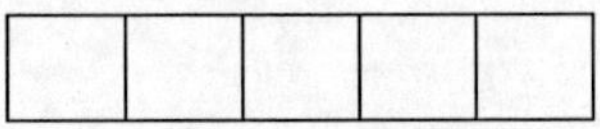

The black nodes still have four blocks.

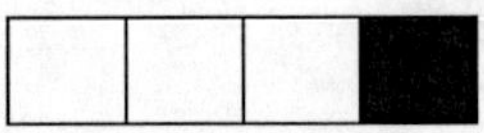

Nakamoto consensus says that accept the longest chain, which represents the most amount of cumulative work done.

Once Block 5 is relayed in the network, all the dark nodes will abandon Block 4 created by Sam and replace it with Lindy's Block 4. Then they will add Block 5 relayed by white nodes. In this way, everyone has accepted the longest chain and agreed on a single blockchain version.

Sam's Block 4 is called 'orphaned' because no one will relay it further. Lindy will be rewarded for creating Block 4 as her block is part of the longest chain.

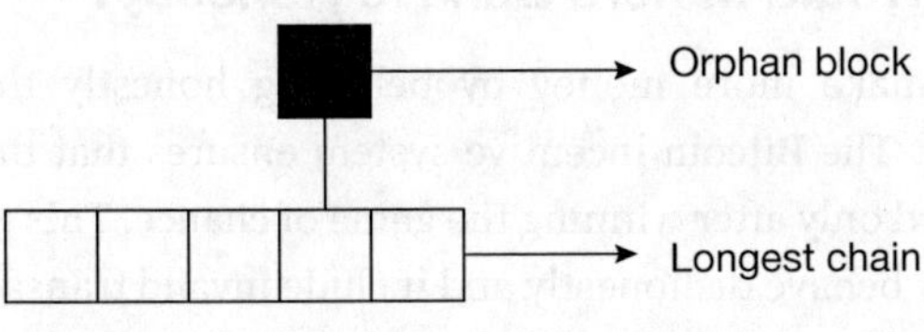

The chain that contains the orphan block is called a 'fork'. It is a subsidiary chain. Ninety-nine per cent of the time, nodes will choose not to continue with a fork. However, there can be deliberate forks resulting in a chain split.

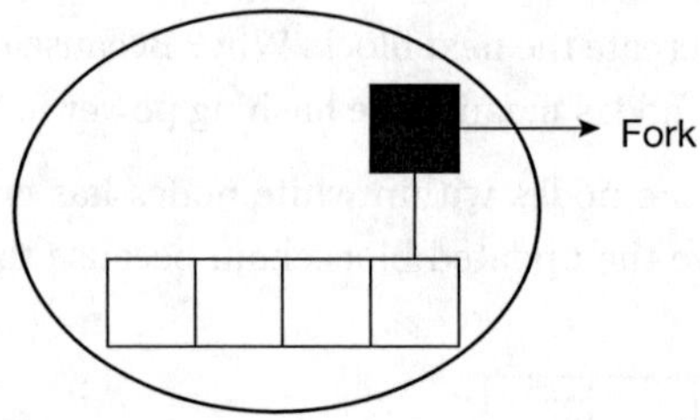

Below you can see that the network has accepted the longest chain. Miners must add new blocks to the longest chain.

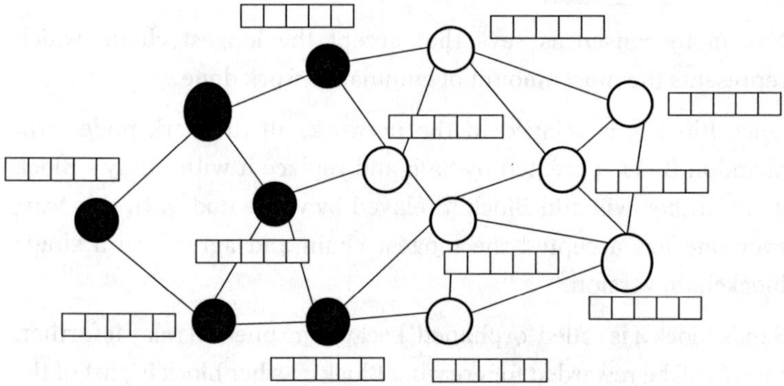

14. Why Would Miners Behave Honestly?

They will make more money by behaving honestly than acting dishonestly. The Bitcoin incentive system ensures that they get the block reward only after winning the game of chance. This game costs a lot. If they behave dishonestly and include invalid transactions in a block or create an invalid block, they will lose money. They will fail to recover the electricity bill and the cost of hardware, as the block will get rejected by others.

15. What Are the Merits and Demerits of POW?

Merits

Block creation: It helps decide who will create the next block. The node which finds the solution to the challenge wins and creates the block.

Order of blocks: It helps maintain the order of the blocks. Do you remember that the previous block hash is included while calculating the block hash in mining? Hence, a chronological order is maintained.

Makes the blockchain immutable: One of the crucial benefits of mining is that it prevents tampering of data in the blockchain. Anyone who changes anything in a previous block must *redo the POW* for all subsequent blocks. Since it takes huge computing power to generate a block hash, it is practically impossible to remine all the existing blocks before an honest block is circulated among participants.

Block reward: The miner who solves the game of luck receives new bitcoins and the transaction fees is included in that block. It provides an incentive to become a miner. Miners are essential for maintaining the integrity of ledger.

Easy verification: The challenge is difficult, but miners can verify it in less than a second. Every node in the network will take the details included in the new block and the nonce generated by the winner and recalculate the block hash to check its validity.

Demerits

One of the biggest demerits of POW is the electricity required for mining. Bitcoin mining consumes electricity equivalent to an average-sized country. It has a detrimental effect on environment. Further, mining power is concentrated wherever electricity is available at less cost. For example, China has become a hub for miners because of cheap electricity. Geographic concentration of miners increases the risk of single point of failure—governments can siege mining rigs and electricity is hampered.

16. What Kind of Devices Are Used for Mining?

When bitcoin was introduced in 2009, the difficulty level was extremely low. It remained low for one to two years; then, people aware of bitcoin used to mine it for fun. They could mine it using regular laptops or PCs running on a central processing unit (CPU), called CPU mining. CPU devices became obsolete as soon as people found out that they could mine better with graphics processing units (GPUs) or computers with a GPU. As more people started mining, the bitcoin mining difficulty went up. Computers with graphics cards were used to accommodate the increased difficulty. The gaming community commonly used these graphics cards to run high-end games. Due to its capacity for parallel processing, it could generate more hashes per second than CPUs. Miners designed specialized motherboards which could work with multiple graphics cards. GPU mining became obsolete with the advent of ASIC.

Note: GPU mining is still helpful in other cryptocurrencies such as Ether.

Around 2013, bitcoin was already well known, and specialized industry-level mining equipment was developed. These devices are known as application-specific integrated circuits or ASIC. Over time, ASIC chips became more and more powerful. Some of the best ASIC mining devices can generate 100 trillion hashes per second. There are mining companies which run thousands of mining rigs. These rigs are built by combining multiple ASICs.

17. Can I Make Money as a Miner in 2022?

Profiting from mining depends on the cost of the mining device, hash rate of the device and cost of electricity in your area. You can use any of the online profitability calculators to see if you will make any profit or not. For example, check out this calculator: https://www.coinwarz.com/mining/bitcoin/calculator. A good ASIC miner with 100 trillion hashes per second would cost you anywhere between $12,000 and $20,000 when writing this book.

For example, assuming you live in the USA where electricity costs around $0.125 KWh (kilowatts per hour) and you have brought the best ASIC miner with 140 TH/s capacity (which can cost you $18,000), you may earn around $21 per day. This is not a guaranteed income, and you have a chance to make consistent money 'only if you join a mining pool' (more on this shortly). You will recover your hardware cost in 857 days or 2.4 years at this rate of profit. If you are lucky and your ASIC is still useful after 2.4 years, you will start to make some actual profit. It will take you 1,384 days to mine 1 bitcoin (at its current price of $42,000). Further, if you are mining on your own, your chance of solving a block is less than winning a lottery. If you win, all is well, but it will cost you your initial investment plus electricity cost if you don't. Therefore, most of the miners are mining through a mining pool.

18. What Are Mining Pools?

It is almost impossible for an individual miner to stumble upon a valid block with the current level of difficulty. Therefore, they join a mining pool. Mining pools work as lottery pools. It is like buying lottery tickets with a group of friends and agreeing to share the prize if any one of you wins. You can share the reward in the proportion of lottery tickets brought by each friend.

Managed Pools

Mining pools are companies which provide a platform for solo miners to do collaborative mining. They maintain the full node of the

Bitcoin Core with the entire blockchain and validate the transactions on behalf of miners. Thousands of miners join the mining pool by downloading specialized software offered by the pool mining company and connecting their hardware to the pool server. This software executes the pool protocols like STM or getblocktemplate protocol (GBT).

The pool server creates a candidate block by collecting transactions from its mempool, calculating the Merkle root of transactions, linking to the previous block hash, and adding a coinbase transaction (with extra nonce space). We have discussed how the extra nonces saved the miners from running out of standard nonces. As the block header contains the metadata of the candidate block, it sends the block header to every pool miner as a template. It also sets a less difficult target hash along with the extremely difficult target hash set by the bitcoin protocol.

Everyone starts mining the candidate block template. They will try to find a hash below the target hash by the bitcoin protocol. In this process, they will generate many hashes smaller than the pool's target hash which is set at a high level (higher hash target means low difficulty). The more hash power a miner has, the more it will hit the target set by the pool. Since mining is a game of luck, any member of the pool will find the target hash set by the bitcoin protocol. Since the coinbase transaction contains the mining company's address, the mining company will receive the new bitcoin and transaction fees.

Everyone will send their block back to the pool company. Its server will check each block to identify how many times the miner has hit the easy target. Since more hash power can result in more hits and less hash power can result in fewer hits, it is a measure of hash power used by the miner. The mining company then distributes the block reward to the pool miners based on the hash power in solving the mining puzzle. Everyone gets some share of the reward even if all of them except one or two fail to stumble upon the golden hash set by bitcoin protocol. Mining pools are open to everyone; hence, many industry-level miners operating thousands of mining rigs also participate in mining pools. Mining pools help in the fair distribution of rewards in exchange for the commission charged to the participant miners.

P2P Pools

There are also decentralized mining pools, but they are not very popular among miners because they require miners to maintain a full blockchain of around 300 GB. In such pools, miners must construct their candidate block. They also create a share chain which is a blockchain at a lower difficulty level. While mining the target hash set by the bitcoin protocol, they would hit the target hash of the share chain more often. Blocks mined at the share chain target are shared in the share chain every 30 seconds. The more the blocks mined in the share chain, the more the share earned by the miner in the ultimate block reward. Suppose one of the miners hits the golden hash set by the bitcoin protocol. The block reward is then shared among all the participants in the proportion of shares earned in the share chain. P2P pools eliminate the need for a centralized authority like a pool mining company. However, centralized mining pools are more popular among miners because of less storage and hardware requirements.

In the below picture, you can see the hash rate distribution of the bitcoin network over four days (at the time of writing this book). Some companies such as AntPool, F2Pool and Poolin control a substantial portion of hash power. Sometimes, these companies temporarily change their tag or input addresses, making them untraceable. However, they cannot be hidden long because of the payouts to pool miners' addresses. These payouts can be linked and tracked by chain analysis.

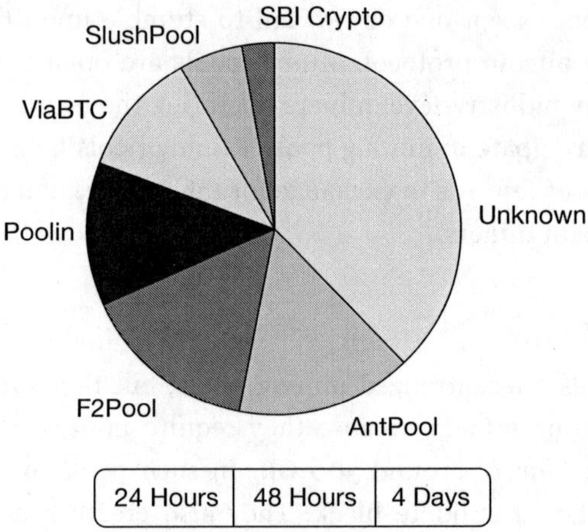

Source: https://www.blockchain.com/charts/pools

19. Why Is Mining Not Required in Permissioned Blockchains?

Permissioned blockchains like private and consortium blockchains don't require mining. These blockchains are used by business enterprises where the identity of the participants is known to every other participant. Hence, instead of using mining or POW, which demands colossal electricity and computational cost, they can follow simpler consensus mechanisms.

20. What Are the Alternatives to POW?

POW is the most decentralized consensus mechanism available to date. It is used by major cryptocurrency blockchains like bitcoin and Ethereum. But since it consumes a lot of electricity and hurts the environment, people have proposed alternative consensus protocols. I will discuss two crucial alternatives to POW. These are alternative solutions to the consensus problem: Who should create the next block?

Proof of Stake

This was proposed in 2011 by a member of the Bitcoin forum. The idea can be summarized as follows:

- Anyone who holds the base cryptocurrency can become a validator.
- A validator's chance of mining a block depends on how much stake they have in that cryptocurrency. For example, if you own 10 per cent of the cryptocurrency, you will be allowed to mine 10 per cent of all its transactions.

There are many benefits of POS. It doesn't require you to spend on electricity and computing power. It is energy efficient. Initiating an attack on the blockchain is expensive. You must have a significant number of cryptocurrencies. There is reduced incentive for the attack. Because you own a majority stake in the cryptocurrency, why would you attack its blockchain? You will lose an enormous amount of wealth. Conversely, large cryptocurrency holders can validate more blocks and create more coins. The richer you are, the richer you become.

Concept note: POS needs POW to generate the coins first. As a blockchain matures and more and more nodes join the network, it can move to a POS-based consensus mechanism. For example, Ethereum, which initially used POW, is now moving into POS.

Proof of Elapsed Time (PoET)

It was proposed by Intel as part of Hyperledger Sawtooth—a blockchain platform for building distributed ledger applications. It states that each participant in the network has to wait for a random amount of time. Each block in the network generates a random time for waiting and going to sleep. The first to wake wins the chance to create the new block. To verify that the proposer has waited for a random amount of time, you must use specialized hardware (SGX) and trusted software manufactured by intel. It is resource-friendly and prevents high energy consumption, but can we fully trust intel's hardware and software? Maybe not.

21. What Is 51 Per Cent attack?

It refers to the double-spend attack or tampering with the bitcoin blockchain by an individual or group controlling more than half of the hashing power. If someone owns more than 51 per cent of hashing power, they can create multiple blocks in a row. They can use it to launch a double-spend attack. For example, assume you have super-fast mining devices which could produce 51 per cent or more hashing power. Since you can mine faster than others, your blockchain would be the longest chain, and as per the Nakamoto consensus, the network should follow the longest chain. Here is how you can carry out a double-spend attack:

1. Keep the longest chain mined by you a secret.
2. Send whatever bitcoins you already own to an exchange, convert them to USD and withdraw them to your bank account.
3. Broadcast your secretly mined longest blockchain to the network.
4. You have rewritten the history in which you never spent any coins on the exchange. You still own the bitcoins, which you can spend again.

However, 51 per cent hashing power will not allow you to do the following:

1. You can't steal others' coins and spend because you can't provide digital signatures.
2. You can't create coins out of thin air.
3. You can't change the rules of Bitcoin.

Although it was difficult to gain 51 per cent control of hash power in 2021, it had happened once in bitcoin history. In 2014, a mining pool named GHash.io exceeded the threshold of 51 per cent briefly. This has forced the Bitcoin community to think seriously about this issue. GHash.io released a voluntary statement promising it would not exceed 40 per cent of hashing power and requested other mining pools to follow the same for the sustainability of the Bitcoin community. In 2015, the hash power of GHash.io had dropped less than 2 per cent of the total hash rate. There is no known solution to a 51 per cent attack; it is unlikely for a pool to gain 51 per cent power as the participants may choose to move out. It is in the interest of the miners to safeguard the blockchain. If protecting something is more beneficial than destroying that thing, we tend to protect that thing (principle of human nature).

20 ECONOMICS

The bitcoin protocol decides bitcoin economics. On the contrary, central banks decide the monetary policy of a country. Central banks issue currencies and then commercial and private banks increase the money supply through credit. Excessive credits can result in bank runs and hyperinflation. We have seen how it has destroyed countries like Zimbabwe, Greece and Venezuela.

Bitcoin is a deflationary coin as there will be only 21 million coins, and the generation of the tokens will decrease over time. Isn't this a good thing? Well, economists are more frightened by deflation than inflation.

Deflation is when there is less money in the system. The price of goods and services falls along with the money supply. If people spend less, companies produce less, and they earn less revenue with less production. They will have to lay off people and shut down factories at some point. Jobless people find it hard to repay their obligations such as home loans, student loans and credit card bills. Banks shut down due to bad debts. Panic spreads, resulting in bank runs. There is less money available to do business. Everyone wants to hold liquid cash due to fear, further reducing production and increasing unemployment. The whole financial system goes numb. This kind of a situation is called recission, and a severe form of recession is called depression.

History has witnessed severe periods of depression caused by deflation, that is, the Great Depression of the USA from 1929 to 1933, deflation in Japan in the mid-1990s and the worldwide recession in 2008. How will bitcoin handle deflation if it wants to become a mainstream currency? Each bitcoin can be divided into 100 million satoshis.

A satoshi is the smallest unit of bitcoin which can be used for the transaction. Therefore, we have 2,100 million or 2.1 billion satoshis. This is still less supply. When the supply of an asset is less (in this case, limited), people often hold it with the hopes of getting rich by capital appreciation instead of spending it. This is what happened with bitcoin. People are using bitcoin more as an investment vehicle rather than money. Most of the investments are speculative. It doesn't seem to match with the vision of Satoshi Nakamoto, who launched it as P2P electronic cash which can substitute the payment mechanism of banks and intermediaries.

Bitcoins are created over a period as per the bitcoin issuance schedule programmed in its protocol. The number of new bitcoins issued to miners is *halved* after every 210,000 blocks, which is around four years. Bitcoin started with generating 50 BTC per creation of the valid block. As of 2022, it is 6.25 BTC per block.

BITCOIN HALVING

Bitcoin has been through three halving as of 2022. The latest halving was triggered on 12 May 2020, as the China-based mining pool called AntPool mined the 630,000th block. With this freshly mined block, block reward had been reduced from 12.5 BTC per block to 6.25 BTC per block. Investors, speculators and the public which had held bitcoin were eagerly waiting for the event with the hope of a price rise. The assumption behind such hopes was that the demand for bitcoin would remain the same, resulting in a price rise as the supply is reduced. Such beliefs are speculative, as the price of an asset depends on the actions of millions of market participants residing over the globe. The demand must translate into people willing to buy the asset at higher prices. To pump the price up, the cumulative buying power must overtake the cumulative selling power. Since buying and selling decisions are impacted by a myriad of factors, including regulatory developments, digital innovations, celebrity hype, media coverage, economic situations, etc., it isn't easy to gauge the price of bitcoin after halving.

However, bitcoin halving doubles the cost of mining. Miners can be thought of as producers of bitcoin. The network must compensate them with higher prices to cover the production cost. Looking back at the 12e-year history of bitcoin, we can see that the last three halving had positively impacted the bitcoin price. The first halving was done in 2012, and bitcoin price skyrocketed, resulting in an 8,069 per cent gain in the next 365 days. It rose 284 per cent within a year from the second halving initiated in 2016. And the third halving, too, didn't disappoint bitcoin holders as the price shot up by 559 per cent within a year from May 2020. This provides us insight into how people react to bitcoin halving as there is a trend of bullish price action followed by such events. The next halving is expected in early 2024, and we will have to wait and see the market's reaction then.[1]

EFFECT OF BITCOIN HALVING ON MINERS

A miner's reward is proportional to its mining capacity. As we have seen, the capacity or hash power of individual miners is tiny compared to a hash pool. When the block reward decreases, miners expect the price to go up so that they can be compensated for the

1 Kevin Groves, 'What Is the Bitcoin Halving? Does It Affect the Price?' 19 March 2022, https://www.hedgewithcrypto.com/what-is-the-bitcoin-halving/

hardware and electricity costs. But as with any asset, prices are subject to ups and downs. Suppose the bitcoin price stays low for an extended period. In that case, small mining farms will find it difficult to recover their cost even if they hit block reward as the quantity is halved. The fear of loss would force small- and medium-sized miners to join mining pools or leave the mining business altogether. This would result in loss of distribution of power and an increase in the concentration of mining power with mining pools. As per the National Bureau of Economic Research, the concentration of mining capacity increases after the bitcoin halving dates, which indicates that the set of large miners is relatively stable. It is the small miners that join and leave in response to price shocks. This increases the risk of a 51 per cent attack.[2]

WILL THERE BE MINERS AFTER THE YEAR 2140?

The issuance of new bitcoins will decrease over time, and it will be zero after the year 2140. Why would there be any miner who put effort into recording others' transactions if there is no incentive? The standard expectation is that transaction fees will fill up the gap of new bitcoins and work as the block reward's sole constituent. The transaction fees must increase to make it equally attractive for miners as any newly mined bitcoin would. This seems highly unlikely. Why would anyone send or receive bitcoin if 90 per cent of coin value would be eroded in transit? And if there are only a handful, why would any person or institution be interested in working as a miner. This will jeopardize the whole bitcoin network, as there will be significantly less hash power to protect the network. Any prominent player would be able to initiate a 51 per cent attack. Here, we can see that maybe Satoshi

2 Igor Makarov and Antoinette Schoar, 'Blockchain Analysis of the Bitcoin Market', NBER, October 2021, https://www.nber.org/system/files/working_papers/w29396/w29396.pdf

Nakamoto's vision was not so visionary after all. In the Bitcoin white paper, he states that one of the significant drawbacks of banks and financial institutions is that the transaction costs are high, making micropayments impossible. But his system would anyway increase the transaction cost far more than any banking system had ever done. The network needs to come out with a solution for this. POW, which consumes a lot of energy, must be substituted by a reliable and less costly consensus protocol such as POS.

21 RULE MAKERS

Bitcoin is a protocol, a set of rules automated by Bitcoin client software. Satoshi Nakamoto had encoded these rules in the first implementation of the bitcoin protocol called Bitcoin Core. The rules have been revised many times, and now there are many versions of Bitcoin Core software. Other implementations are also there, as everyone is free to write their software, as long as the software follows the rules that everyone is following. Since these rules dictate what constitutes a valid block and what is not, you would like to run the Bitcoin Core implementation that most of the users are running. This ensures that your blocks don't get invalidated by others just because of coding bugs. Millions of users, thousands of miners, hundreds of exchanges and e-commerce providers run some form of bitcoin node. But who makes the amendments or improvements to the bitcoin protocol and how are these amendments done?

BITCOIN IMPROVEMENT PROPOSALS

Bitcoin Core software is not owned and controlled by any single organization. Instead, it is managed by the Bitcoin community. All changes to the protocol are agreed to be proposed as a bitcoin improvement proposal (BIP). This is how a BIP is executed.

1. Proposal: Anyone from the community can submit a proposal for improving the existing software. They should first check with the community whether such proposals have been considered and rejected before. Going through all the past BIPs listed in GitHub[1] is recommended. They should then discuss the idea in appropriate forums to build community consensus for the BIP.

2. Draft: Once the author is satisfied that their idea is novel and has community support, they should send a draft to the Bitcoin development mailing list. It should be well formatted, of high quality and address additional BIP concerns.

3. Review: Once the editors review the draft BIP, it will be assigned a number and submitted to the GitHub repository of BIPs.

BIPs are rejected on the ground of duplication of effort, poor formatting, unclear or too broad, technically unsound, not having backward compatibility or deviating from the core philosophy of Bitcoin. To be accepted, it should fulfil minimum criteria such as having a clear and complete description of the improvement, not creating unnecessary complications in the protocol and the enhancement must represent a net improvement.

4. Finalization: It becomes final based on real-world adaptability. There is no formal voting, and users show their agreement by running the software of their choice. For example, it is final if past 2016 blocks have been mined through the software that implements the rules of the new BIP.

You can read more about the process here: bips/bip-0002.mediawiki at master · bitcoin/bips · GitHub

Money does not have any value if it has no users, if no one accepts it for the exchange of goods. Hence, whether a change to the protocol would be successful or not depends on those willing to offer goods, services and other currencies in exchange for bitcoin. These are the users, constituting merchants and buyers, and often referred to as the *economic majority,* who ultimately use bitcoin to fulfil some

1 Bitcoin/BIPs, https://github.com/bitcoin/bips

economic purpose. Every user within the economic majority decides what they consider is bitcoin. And all of them stick to the bitcoin invented by Satoshi. Therefore, all bitcoin changes must be approved by the users. It is impossible to force your rules on everyone without their consent. For example, *even if 100 per cent of* miners collude and decide to use software that rewards them more bitcoin per block, other users such as exchanges, merchants and the public will reject the bitcoin created by those blocks. They will dump the currency, dragging the price down and making it worthless. If developers want to enforce radical changes to the software that the rest of the community does not like, their changes would be rejected by others. Therefore, it is the ultimate users of bitcoin that decide the rules. This was made clear in 2017, when BIP 148 was implemented.

BIP 148: SEGREGATED WITNESS

Each transaction in bitcoin has a space, called the witness portion, which contains digital signatures used for validating the authenticity of transactions. The proposal was to segregate the witness portion from transaction data so that transactions' size can be reduced, which will, in turn, reduce the block size. Technically speaking, the witness data would be excluded from the Merkle tree and separately included in the block header. The proposal was first initiated by Bitcoin Core developer Pieter Wuille in 2015 through BIP 141. Later, BIP 143 and 144 added some improvements to it.

However, miners blocked the implementation of SegWit during 2015 and 2016. In February 2017, a pseudonymous user called 'Shaolin Fry' posted BIP 148, in which he requested the economic majority to activate SegWit. He described the motivation behind such proposal as follows:

> SegWit increases the block size, fixes transaction malleability, and makes scripting easier to upgrade as well as bringing many other benefits. It is hoped that miners will respond to this BIP by activating

SegWit early before this BIP takes effect. Otherwise, this BIP will cause the **mandatory activation** (emphasis by the author) of the existing SegWit deployment before the end of midnight November 15th, 2017.[2]

If the economy decided to activate SegWit, everyone would have ignored the transactions and blocks that didn't follow the new rules. Miners could break the new rules if they wanted to. Still, it is in their interest to avoid approving invalid transactions and blocks. The block reward wouldn't have any value in the Bitcoin ecosystem, which considers those blocks invalid. Eventually, SegWit was activated by the community with a backward-compatible mode. Both SegWit and non-SegWit blocks were deemed valid. Although SegWit adoption was initially low, it is more than 80 per cent at the time of writing this book.

You can find the whole list of BIPs in the GitHub repository.

2 bips/bip-0148.mediawiki, shaolinfry Update BIP status, Motivation, https://github.com/bitcoin/bips/blob/master/bip-0148.mediawiki

PART 4
Crypto World

22 DIGITAL CURRENCIES

Cryptocurrencies are a specific type of digital currency. We must be aware of the whole spectrum of digital currencies to understand the place and relevance of cryptocurrencies.

WHAT IS DIGITAL CURRENCY?

It is a kind of currency stored and exchanged on digital computer systems, especially via the Internet. It exists only in electronic form. There are two major types of digital currencies based on their source of issuance (Figure 22.1).

In the digital currency tree, you can see that there are broadly three types of digital currency based on centralization.

1. Fully centralized digital currencies
2. Partially decentralized digital currencies
3. Fully decentralized digital currencies

FULLY CENTRALIZED DIGITAL CURRENCIES

These are electronic representations of money *issued by* a central administrator and *transacted via* centralized networks, where a trusted intermediary clears and settles transactions. Since issuance, storage and maintenance are controlled by a central agency, we can

Figure 22.1 Digital Currency Tree

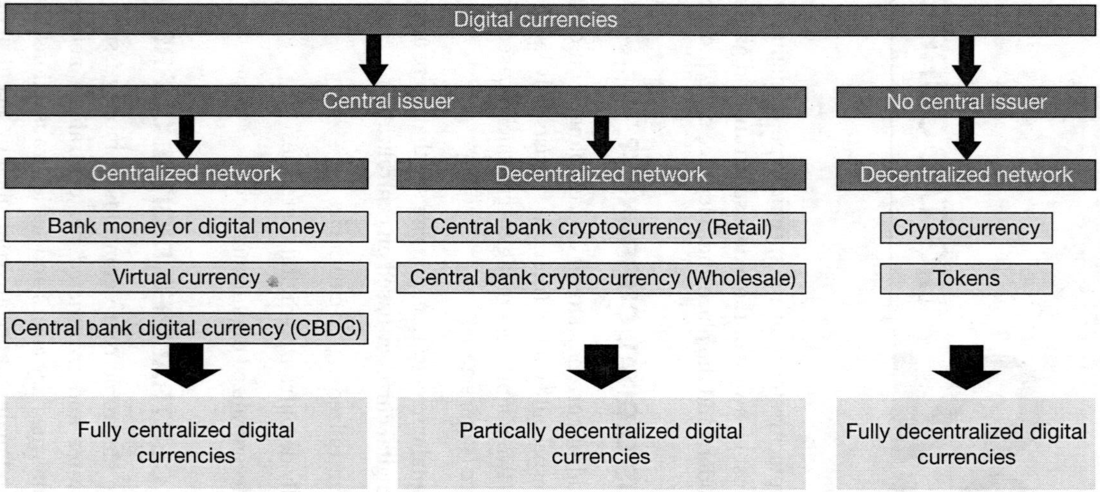

call these *fully centralized digital currencies*. You can identify two levels of control in the digital currency tree represented by circles. There are four broad types of fully centralized digital currencies.

Central Bank Deposits

These are central bank deposits held by commercial banks—often referred to as settlement accounts or reserves. These are kept in the digital ledgers of the central bank.

Commercial and Private Bank Deposits

These are customer deposits stored in the digital ledgers of the commercial and private banks. These constitute a substantial portion of the digital currency we have today.

Virtual Currencies

As per the European central bank, 'A virtual currency is a type of unregulated, digital money, which is issued and usually controlled by its developers, and used and accepted among the members of a specific virtual community.'[1] Gaming communities mostly use these currencies to make in-game purchases.[2] For Example, PokéCoin is a currency used for in-game purchases in the Pokémon Go game. World of Warcraft (WoW) Gold is a virtual currency used in this well-known online role-playing game designed by Blizzard Entertainment. The game developing company issues and regulates these currencies; these have no utility outside the gaming community. Virtual currencies also include digital coupons which users can redeem for real-life goods and services. Once the coupon is used, it cannot

1 ECB (2012).

2 Morten Bech and Rodney Garratt, 'Central Bank Cryptocurrencies', September 2017, https://www.bis.org/publ/qtrpdf/r_qt1709f.pdf

be exchanged back to the digital coupons. Hence, these are called currencies with a *unidirectional flow* of value.[3]

Example: Amazon Pay coupons

Central Bank Digital Currencies

There are public deposit accounts with the central bank. Central bank accounts are usually available for commercial banks and financial institutions. However, it is possible to allow the public to open a central bank account with present-day technology. While the idea is old, central banks have refrained from issuing such accounts to people.[4]

PARTIALLY DECENTRALIZED DIGITAL CURRENCIES

These are the partially decentralized counterparts of central bank digital currency (CBDC).

> **Central bank cryptocurrency (retail):** CBCC retail will be used by the public.[5]
> **Central bank cryptocurrency (wholesale):** CBCC wholesale will be used by financial institutions.[6]

FULLY DECENTRALIZED DIGITAL CURRENCIES

These currencies are neither issued by a central administer nor controlled by a centralized network. Both issuance and control over the network are decentralized.

3 European Central Bank, 'Virtual Currency Schemes—A Further Analysis', February 2015, https://www.ecb.europa.eu/pub/pdf/other/virtualcurrencyschemesen.pdf
4 Bech and Garratt, 'Central Bank Cryptocurrencies'.
5 Ibid.
6 Ibid.

There are two variants of this kind of money.

1. Cryptocurrencies: These are digital currencies essential for the functioning of blockchain-based systems. We have discussed bitcoin in Part 3. In the next chapter, we will have an overview of alternative coins and tokens.

2. Crypto tokens: These are digital currencies created on top of an existing system for monetary or other purposes. The system doesn't rely on tokens to function.

23 ALTCOINS

There are thousands of cryptocurrencies developed over the last decade. As I write this book, over 10,000 are traded in various crypto exchanges worldwide.[1] It is impossible to talk about the intricacies of all these cryptocurrencies. Instead, we can focus on the commonalities or the broad technical differences. All these currencies can be grouped under two categories: altcoins and tokens.

ALTCOINS

An altcoin is simply an abbreviation for 'alternative coins'. These coins refer to the currencies which have been created 'after bitcoin as an alternative to bitcoin'.

We can classify altcoins into four categories:

1. Some are created by splitting the bitcoin blockchain and are commonly referred to as hard forks.
2. Some are copies of bitcoin.
3. Some are created independently from the Bitcoin codebase but still use a blockchain-based system. One of the prominent examples is Ether.

1 Raynor de Best, 'Number of Cyptocurrencies Worldwide from 2013 to February 2022', https://www.statista.com/statistics/863917/number-crypto-coins-tokens/; Raynor de Best, 'Quantity of cryptocurrencies as of February 3,2022', https://www.statista.com/statistics/863917/number-crypto-coins-tokens/

4. Some are created independently from Bitcoin but don't use a blockchain-based system.

Bitcoin Forks

Forks are changes to bitcoin protocol. There are two types of forks.

Soft forks: These changes are backward compatible. It allows nodes to ignore the new changes and continue with the old version. These nodes will consider the blocks mined under new rules as valid. Soft forks don't result in altcoins. For example, SegWit was a soft fork.

Hard forks: These changes are not backward compatible. The nodes must choose between old rules and new rules. Nodes which stick to the old rules will consider the coins generated under the new rules invalid. If the new protocol gets some traction, it will result in a chain split: the old chain that runs the older version of the software and the new chain that uses the latest software. Both the blockchains will share the same history up to the point of separation and record different sets of blocks after the split. Coins generated by both blockchains will be different. The question is: Which set of coins gets to retain the old name. The community waits for 2016 blocks to observe which chain has the highest hash rate. The winning chain keeps the old name; the losing chain will have a different name, and coins mined under this would be considered altcoins.

Example: Bitcoin Cash

In 2016, Mike Hearn, a former Google engineer and Bitcoin developer, called Bitcoin a failed experiment, citing various reasons such as inability to handle more transactions, unpredictable fees, long waiting time and concentration of mining power with few mining pools. He went on to hard fork Bitcoin in 2017 and created a new coin called Bitcoin Cash which accepts large block sizes to process more transactions. Both Bitcoin and Bitcoin Cash share the same genesis block and same history until the point of splitting. One Bitcoin Cash was trading around $300 at the time of writing this book.

Bitcoin Cash was itself hard forked in 2018 by a notorious figure called Craig Wright, who considered it to have deviated far from the initial vision of Satoshi. The coin was called Bitcoin Satoshi Vision or Bitcoin SV. One Bitcoin SV was trading around $90 when writing this book.

Copies of Bitcoin

One of the easiest ways to create an altcoin is to take the Bitcoin codebase, change some parameters and relaunch it with some different name. Some call these code forks. Unlike hard forks, these coins don't share any history with the bitcoin blockchain. Notable examples include Ixcoin, GeistGaid, Solidcoin, Namecoin and Primecoin. Most of these failed to gain a user base except a few.

Litecoin

It was developed by Charlie Lee in 2011, who was a developer at Google then. Charlie noticed that most of the altcoins failed because the developers remained anonymous and held pre-mined coins (pre-mined coins are the coins which are mined before the blockchain goes live). Pseudonymity worked for Satoshi because he was the original inventor of something groundbreaking. Unlike Satoshi, the founders of these coins were changing the parameters of existing innovation. People found it difficult to trust such projects. The developers could sell their share of currency and walk away anytime. Considering all these factors, Charlie decided to create a lighter version of bitcoin with four times the supply of bitcoin and four times faster block creation time. He refrained from pre-mining Litecoin and decided to use Scrypt instead of the SHA 256 algorithm for POW mining. Litecoin was ranked at #21 in terms of market capitalization, and one Litecoin was priced around $100 at the time of writing this book.

Dogecoin

Dogecoin was created as a joke by Billy Markus and Jackson Palmer in 2013. It was their way to mock the grand promises made by bitcoin and other cryptocurrencies. They chose the famous doge meme as their logo, creating the world's first meme-based cryptocurrency called meme coins. It featured the face of a Shiba Inu dog with a comic appearance. Billy and Palmer modified the Litecoin parameters to create Dogecoin. It used the Scrypt algorithm for mining. One block takes around one minute to mine and generates 10,000 Dogecoins. Hence, 5 billion new dogecoins are added every year. Although the supply of Dogecoins was capped at 100 billion initially, it was removed after a community discussion.

Soon after its launch, it became a famous currency backed by a strong community. In December 2020, Elon Musk tweeted about Dogecoin, which attracted worldwide attention. Musk continued to support it through his tweets, and by May 2021, it had risen by 20,000 per cent in a single year. It surpassed the market capitalization of $50 billion and became the fifth-largest cryptocurrency. While writing this book, it is ranked 11th place and has a market capitalization of $16 billion.

Independent of Bitcoin

These are the altcoins that bitcoin had inspired, but the codes are not copied or forked from bitcoin.

Ethereum

It is the platform that enables the world's second-largest cryptocurrency, Ether, to function. Ethereum has unleashed the era of blockchain 2.0, allowing it to achieve functionalities beyond running a currency system.

Cardano (ADA)

it was co-founded by Charles Hoskinson, who was one of the founding members of Ethereum. Charles wasn't happy about how Ethereum was progressing; hence, he decided to leave the Ethereum Foundation to build a new blockchain. Cardano is based on extensive research carried out by a team of engineers, mathematicians and cryptologists who have published 120 papers on blockchain technology. It follows POS mining. It is often referred to as Ethereum killer because its proponents believe that it is much more competent than the former. Cardano is the world's sixth-largest cryptocurrency with around $35 billion market capitalization.

Polkadot

It was founded by Gavin Wood, one of the founders of Ethereum. Like the founder of Cardano, Gavin disagreed with the course Ethereum was taking. Polkadot enables the *cross-blockchain transfer* of digital data, including cryptocurrencies. You can interoperate on various blockchains by connecting to the Polkadot platform. It also provides the facility to create new blockchains backed by Polkadot's security protocol. Ethereum provides this facility too, but users need to set their security measures which can be compromised when a project is in its infancy. Since Polkadot is a mature blockchain, it is much more secure. Users don't need to worry about security when starting with a new blockchain. Its governance is user-driven, and upgrades are done by community coordination.

Polkadot has its cryptocurrency called Dot. Dot is *not minable* and has a 10 million supply. However, after a redenomination voting in July 2020, the supply increased to 1 billion Dots. Polkadot follows the POS consensus mechanism, which allows users to cast votes in the proportion of their holding to participate in the decision-making process. When writing this book, a DOT was trading around $17, and it was ranked 10th with around $17 billion market capitalization.

Solana

Solana is viewed as the long-term rival of Ethereum. It enables smart contracts like Ethereum. It uses *both POS and proof of history* consensus mechanisms to agree on the ledger's state. It can handle around 50,000 transactions per second which are far beyond the capacity of Ethereum. SOL is its native cryptocurrency. Each SOL was priced around $100, and it was ranked at #7 at the time of writing this book.

Monero

A paper was published in 2013, which described privacy and anonymity as the most critical aspect of cryptocurrencies, and bitcoin is flawed as it fails to provide complete anonymity. The author of this paper is assumed to be pseudonymous and goes by the name Nicolas van Saberhagen. Nicolas has described a protocol which will provide complete anonymity of transactions through concepts such as ring signatures, zero-knowledge proofs and IP address obscuring. A Bitcointalk forum user called 'tankful for today' created a coin out of this protocol and named it Bitmonero. Monero was created by hard forking Bitmonero in 2014. Monero uses POW-based mining protocol called 'RandomX'. This is ASIC resistant, which discourages large companies from participating in the mining process. Mining can be done using GPU-enabled laptops and PCs. It has a massive community of developers only below the Bitcoin and Ethereum. The development team is primarily anonymous. Due to its anonymity mechanism, criminals use it for paying for illicit products on the darknet. Coinhive, a malware developed by hackers, could be embedded in websites and apps, which would then drain the CPU power of visitors to mine Monero for the hackers. Hackers also preferred to receive payment in Monero in case of ransomware attacks. Because of increased criminal activity, some of the exchanges delisted Monero. US Internal Revenue Service (IRS) Criminal Investigation Division announced a bounty for contractors who can develop tools to track transactions done in Monero and other so-called 'privacy coins' like Dash. When writing this book, Monero had a market capitalization of $2 billion, which placed it on 43rd rank.

Non-blockchain Currencies

As discussed previously, a blockchain is only one kind of DLT. Cryptocurrencies may choose to use a DLT method without using blockchain. One such notable currency is IOTA.

IOTA

From the Internet of information, we are moving towards the Internet of things, a network of intelligent devices capable of communicating with each other. We may see devices engaging in economic transactions soon. For example, a smart automatic car can accept bookings, pick up and drop passengers, receive payment, and pay for fuel and maintenance charges on its own. There is a need for a worldwide ledger or ledger of everything to enable such transactions. Here is where IOTA comes into the picture. It claims to be the first distributed ledger built for everything and a network exchanging value and data between humans and machines. There are no blocks, no miners and no transaction fees. Anyone who sends a transaction needs to validate two other transactions. This is how IOTA plans to overcome the scalability and cost issues of bitcoin and Ethereum. Unlike the blockchain, it uses directed acyclic graph (DAG) data structure to record transactions parallelly. Its network is called tangle, which ensures that data is stored in an immutable record. IOTA transactions are confirmed within minutes.

IOTA has been criticized for its unusual design, and claims are yet to be proved. Its decentralization claim falls apart because it requires a coordinator node to operate, controlled by the IOTA foundation. This makes it centralized, and the coordinator is vulnerable as a single point of failure. It was compromised in 2018 when around $10 of IOTA tokens were stolen from 85 users. It was again hacked in 2019, resulting in a theft of $2 million worth of IOTA tokens. IOTA 2.0, called Coordicide, announced in 2020, aims to function without a coordinator node. There is a fixed supply of 2,779,530,283,277,761 IOTA tokens in circulation. When writing this book, it was ranked 48th, with a market capitalization of $2.1 billion.

TOKENS

Altcoins are native cryptocurrencies which are *essential for the functioning* of the blockchain system. Unlike altcoins, crypto *tokens* are created on top of the existing system. These may or may not be used for monetary purposes. Hence, even if the tokens disappear, the blockchain would still function. Ethereum is the most preferred platform to launch new crypto tokens. However, there are some alternative platforms such as Binance and Solana.

Initial Coin Offerings

Tokens have been used to raise funds for new projects. For example, suppose someone has a great idea. They describe their idea in a white paper, specifying the benefits it would create once it is launched. They then create some tokens using Ethereum and offer them to the public in exchange for access to the exclusive facilities that the project will deliver. These facilities may come in the form of rights in the decision-making, access to products or services it offers, etc. Such a public offering of crypto tokens is called initial coin offering (ICO).

ICOs gained popularity during the 2017 cryptocurrency boom. Some of these ICOs survived and became successful projects, but most failed to deliver. Some of them were Ponzi schemes which defrauded millions of dollars from investors. Soon US Securities and Exchange Commission (SEC) took note of these and tightened the regulatory requirements. ICOs are a thing of the past now. They are replaced by initial exchange offerings (IEOs), where tokens are offered through *centralized exchanges* that verify the legitimacy of projects. For example, the Binance exchange is the most popular platform for IEO. It launched its first IEO in 2019, which offered BitTorrent Tokens (BTT). Tokens were sold out in less than 15 minutes and raised over $7.1 million.

Types of Tokens

Tokens can be categorized based on their function within the project. Here are a few broad types of tokens.

Utility Tokens

These tokens provide access to utility within or outside the project. For example, Filecoin is a decentralized cloud storage platform which offers storage facilities in exchange for filecoin tokens.

Security Tokens

These tokens promise a return on investment. Therefore, these ICOs are similar to financial securities such as stocks and bonds. Holding a security token provides you a share in the future payout of the blockchain project.

Native Tokens

Cryptocurrencies are also referred to as native tokens. They are essential for the functioning of their ecosystem, for example, bitcoin and Ether.

Meme Tokens

Meme tokens or meme coins became extremely popular in 2021 following the meteoric rise of Dogecoin. Thousands of dog-themed tokens popped up, claiming to be the next Dogecoin. The Shiba Inu token is the most successful meme coin after Dogecoin. The coin was launched on the Ethereum platform in 2020 with a quadrillion supply. Its founder Ryoshi, who remains anonymous to date, dubbed Shib as the doge killer. The coin came into the limelight when Ryoshi transferred 500 billion tokens to Vitalik Buterin, co-founder of Ethereum. The Ethereum founder then donated 10 per cent of tokens to the COVID relief fund of India and burned the rest of the coins (sent to an unspendable address). A tweet from Elon Musk that featured a Shiba Inu dog helped the coin gain popularity, though Elon denied holding Shiba tokens later. The coin had risen a whopping 121 million per cent as of 27 October 2021. A $1,000 investment in Shiba Inu could have made you a billionaire within a year. It ranked among the top 10 cryptocurrencies with a $40 billion market cap, leaving Dogecoin behind. However, when writing this book, its price has dropped more than 50 per cent from its peak and is placed at 14th rank.

Fungible and Non-fungible Tokens

Fungible tokens are interchangeable with one another and have equal value. At the same time, a non-fungible token (NFT) is unique. Before blockchain, it was impossible to own a digital asset on the Internet. Digital things are, by nature, copiable. However, with blockchain, we can prove the ownership of digital items. You can now own stuff on the Internet. Digital art, photos, videos and paintings can be stored within blockchain with a unique hash. NFTs became immensely popular in 2021, some selling for millions of dollars. Blockchain has paved the way for metaverse, a virtual world where you can own things, including virtual lands.

Platforms

Ethereum is the most used and secure platform for creating tokens. Tokens are made by following Ethereum Request for Comments (ERC) standards. ERC-20 is used for creating fungible tokens, whereas ERC-721 is used for NFTs. ERC-777 is an improved version of ERC-20 and is considered the next-generation standard for issuing fungible tokens.

24 ETHEREUM

Vitalik Buterin, then aged 17, was involved with the Bitcoin community and was an editor of the *Bitcointalk* magazine. He realized that the bitcoin blockchain is underutilized. If we can store transactions in the blockchain, why can't we store instructions? It will make the codes immutable and secure. These codes can do anything that an Android or IOS app can do. With these thoughts in mind, he proposed modifications to Bitcoin to enhance its flexibility. However, the community rejected his proposal. He decided to go on his own and created the conceptual framework for a new kind of blockchain.

Vitalik published a white paper in 2013 which outlined how this new system, called Ethereum, would work. Dr Gavin Wood, one of the founders of Ethereum, published a technical yellow paper in 2014. The project was crowdfunded. An online sale of 72 million *premined* Ether tokens took place during July and August 2014. People made payment trough bitcoins. More than 31,500 BTC, which were worth around $18 million, were raised. The fund was put to use, and Ethereum went live on 30 July 2015.

Ethereum is managed by a community of developers who have launched several updates since its first release. The updates bear interesting names like Android versions.

Ethereum protocol updates		
Code name	**Release date**	**Release bloack**
Frontier	30-Jul-15	0
Ice age	08-Sep-15	200,000
Homestead	15-Mar-16	1,150,000
DAO fork	20-Jul-16	1,920,000
Tangerine whistle	18-Oct-16	2,463,000
Spurious dragon	23-Nov-16	2,675,000
Byzantium	16-Oct-17	4,370,000
Constantinople	28-Feb-19	7,280,000
St. Petersburg	28-Feb-19	7,280,000
Istanbul	08-Dec-19	9,069,000
Muir glacier	02-Jan-20	9,200,000
Berlin	15-Apr-21	12,244,000
London	05-Aug-21	12,965,000

SIMILARITIES BETWEEN BITCOIN AND ETHEREUM

Ethereum Has a Permissionless Blockchain

Similar to bitcoin, Ethereum's blockchain is permissionless. It is open to public. Anyone can join the network by downloading an open-source software.

It Has a Cryptocurrency

Both Bitcoin and Ethereum have their own native tokens. Ethereum's cryptocurrency is called 'Ether' or ETH.

It Uses POW for Mining

Ethereum also follows POW for mining. Its POW algorithm is called Ethash. It is ASIC resistant and intends to increase participation of small miners. However, Ethereum is moving away from POW to POS. This transition is called Ethereum 2.0 is and planned to be competed in three phases.

MOVING BEYOND BITCOIN

From Transactions to Smart Contracts

Transaction: It is an asset transfer between participants. For example, Jack gave his truck to Bob.

Contract: It is a set of one or more conditions for a transaction to occur. For example, If Bob pays Jack, then car is transferred to Bob. Bitcoin allowed only monetary transactions. However, Ethereum was designed to support monetary transactions as well as smart contracts.

Smart Contracts

Contracts specify the conditions for transactions. All conditions can be expressed in the language 'if this, then that'. These kinds of statements can be easily converted into a computer code which executes automatically when the condition is met.

A simple example of a smart contract is a vending machine. If you give it money, it gives you a drink of your choice. There is nothing smart about it; it is just executing the instructions. The term 'smart contract' is a misnomer. It is nothing but a general-purpose computer program.

Let's take a little advanced example.

You have a brilliant project in mind, but you don't have money. You can use a crowdfunding platform like Kickstarter. You will pitch your idea in their website and people who believe in your project will fund you. Kickstarter will release you the funds based on the completed project milestones.

The problem with this kind of arrangement is 'trust'. You and the supporters need to trust the crowdfunding platform. What if the platform owner runs away with money, or what if it is hacked? This is where Ethereum provides a solution.

- The contract is converted into a code which auto-executes when one or more conditions are met. For example, if you achieve milestone 1, then transfer 1,000 ETH. If you fail to achieve milestone 1, then return the money to supporters.
- The computer program is then verified and executed by thousands of miners who record the progress in the Ethereum blockchain.

Smart contracts have three main advantages.

Immutable: Since they are stored in the blockchain, no one can change the terms of the contract and no one can alter the progress.

Decentralized: There is no single point of authority who can tamper with the program.

Distributed: Since every node in the network runs and stores the computer, there is no single point of failure. It is resistant to hacking, server failure and censorship.

Decentralized Apps

When you use Twitter or YouTube, you are bound by the terms and conditions of the company that owns these. Sometimes these conditions are not fair, sometimes these are misused and you can be punished for not following *their rules*. The idea behind decentralized apps is to provide services without censorship. Dapps are extensions of smart contracts. Smart contracts are used for back-end processing, and a user interface is provided so that users can carry out various tasks.

A Global Computer

Ethereum is a global computer which runs in thousands of nodes. What does it mean? All nodes run the same programs and maintain a single state of outcome. They maintain an identical copy of blockchain that contains the following:

- History of all transactions
- History of all smart contracts
- Current state of all smart contracts

Problems

1. What if someone creates a program which can access your private data and infect your computer?
2. What if someone creates a program which runs forever and releases into the network? These kinds of programs can be easily created with infinite loops. Such programs can sabotage the time and resource of thousands of computers.

Ethereum solves the problem of privacy by introducing a virtual computer known as Ethereum virtual machine (EVC). Think of this as a computer within the computer. All the nodes use EVC to run smart contracts and Dapps. What happens within EVC stays within EVC. The programs cannot access anything outside the boundary of EVC. Therefore, the private data of nodes remain safe.

The problem of heavy programs which can halt the network is solved by introducing gas. As you know, a program is just a set of instructions. Gas is the cost you need to pay for each instruction. The more instructions your program has, more cost you need to bear. Hence, a malicious program which can hamper the functioning of network would cost you a lot of money as it will be computationally heavy to execute. If you don't have the gas to pay for it, it will stop running.

ELEMENTS OF ETHEREUM

Ethereum Client Software

There are three official Ethereum full nodes:

1. Geth
2. Eth
3. Pyethapp

Apart from these, an open-source software called Parity developed by Parity Technologies is widely used.

Block

Ethereum blocks are mined in every 14 seconds. This is extremely fast compared to bitcoin, which takes around 10 minutes to mine one block. Because of this, orphan blocks are common in Ethereum blockchain. These blocks are called 'uncle blocks'. Transactions that end up in uncle blocks are remined later and included in blockchain. Users don't need to pay more gas for this.

Ether

Ether is the native cryptocurrency of Ethereum platform. Its supply is not capped like bitcoin. However, only 18 million ETH can be mined per year. Unlike Bitcoin, ETH supply is not halved. The smallest unit of Ether is called Wei. One ETH has 1,000,000,000,000,000,000 Wei. A Giga Wei is 1 billon Wei. Gas prices are expressed in GWei.

Block Reward

Ethereum pays 3 ETH for mining a block. While bitcoin doesn't pay reward for orphan blocks, Ethereum does. If a later block includes an uncle, the miner gets a reward called 'uncle reward'. The miner who includes it also gets a small reward called 'uncle reference reward'. Miners also receive the mining fees which is gas price multiplied by gas consumed.

Gas Price

It is the amount of ETH *per unit of gas* you are prepared to pay to the miners to process your transaction. Think of it as petrol price. The quantity of petrol required for a vehicle to travel certain kilometres remains same despite of the fluctuation in petrol price. For example, a transaction may cost you 100 gas. You can decide how much Wei you want to pay for 100 gas units.

Gas Limit

It is the maximum quantity of gas you want to spend in a transaction. Setting a gas limit puts a cap on your mining fees. For example, it saves you from overpaying mining fees in case you have submitted a complex code by mistake.

Accounts

Ethereum doesn't follow the UTXO model of Bitcoin. It follows a simple account-based system to maintain ledgers. An Ethereum account is similar to a bank account. There are two types of Ethereum accounts.

Externally Owned Accounts

These accounts are used for sending and receiving ETH. Similar to Bitcoin, you need to authenticate a payment by signing it with your private key.

Contract Accounts

If you want to run a smart contract, you must follow two steps:

1. Upload it to an account by sending it to the miners. Once miners validate, it stays in the contract account.
2. Create another transaction, requesting miners to run it from the contract account.

LIFE CYCLE OF AN ETHEREUM TRANSACTION

The transaction process of Ethereum is similar to Bitcoin.

1. You open your wallet and enter the address of the payee and amount of ETH you want to transfer.
2. Your wallet digitally signs the transaction and broadcasts it to the P2P network.
3. Once it reaches the miners, they include it into a candidate block and start to solve POW puzzle.
4. If a miner solves the puzzle, it shares the block with their peers immediately.
5. All the nodes check whether the block is valid. If it is valid, they add it to their copy of blockchain.
6. The payee receives the amount and the miner is rewarded.

25 CBDC

As the cryptocurrency market storms the world by crossing 2 trillion US dollars, central banks worldwide are trying to develop their version of digital currency. While the crypto community frowns on CBDC as these are against the core principles of decentralization, commercial and private banks are worried, as it may lead to disintermediation of banks. These currencies seek to take advantage of the technological breakthroughs and the underlying mechanism of cryptocurrencies.

CBDC SCHEMES

Several design choices are available for central banks based on factors such as accessibility and anonymity.

CBDC (Fully Centralized)

Whenever you deposit money in a bank, it provides you a 'deposit account'. This ledger account is an asset for you but a liability for banks. These can come in two forms.[1]

An account with the central bank (wholesale): Presently, only commercial banks and certain financial institutions can

1 Bech and Garratt, 'Central Bank Cryptocurrencies'.

maintain accounts with the central bank. Therefore, it is already available.

An account with the central bank (retail): These are called digital currency accounts (DCAs). The idea behind this form of CBDC is to issue *general-purpose accounts* to the public. In this way, the public can hold central bank liabilities directly. The benefit is that the central bank is more likely to meet its obligations than a commercial bank. As we have seen, banks can go bankrupt, which puts your money at risk. However, your money is safe with the central bank. The concept of DCA is old, and no central bank has issued these until the Bahamas issued the sand dollar in 2020.[2]

CBDC (Partially Decentralized)

Central banks issue physical tokens such as cash and banknotes. This represents the liability of the central bank towards the public. Therefore, the only way for the public to hold a central bank liability is to have cash. Unlike bank accounts, cash provides counterparty anonymity. It eliminates the counterparty risk such as identity theft, hacking and spamming. This kind of CBDC can provide some degree of anonymity by enabling P2P *digital cash* transfer.

CBCC (retail): These are cryptocurrencies issued by the central bank to the general public. Central banks of different countries may use varied parameters while deciding their CBCC. For example, they must determine the degree of anonymity they want to provide. They may opt for a permissionless blockchain if they wish their CBCC to behave just like cash. Suppose they think that a completely permissionless blockchain is not feasible and the cost of anonymity is more than the benefits. In that case, they can go for a permissioned blockchain with approved banks or third parties as verifiers. Even in a permissioned blockchain,

2 Digital Bahamian Dollar, https://www.sanddollar.bs/

they could make P2P transactions anonymous and keep the user identity accessible to only trusted verifiers. This will reduce the counterparty risk as well as the risk of money laundering and criminal activities.[3]

CBCC (Wholesale): CBCC wholesale is a cryptocurrency which can be issued only to the banks and financial institutions through a permissioned blockchain. It will make the transactions faster, secure and transparent.[4]

PRESENT STATUS OF CBDCs

The following countries have started implementing at least a pilot CBDC. The Bahamas and Nigeria have already launched their CBDCs. Eighty countries are experimenting with CBDC at present.[5]

1. Nigeria has *launched* eNaira.
2. The Bahamas has *launched* sand dollar.
3. China is carrying pilot run for e-CNY.
4. Saudi Arabia is running a pilot for Aber.
5. The USA is doing a pilot run for Jasper.
6. Uruguay has launched a pilot run for e-Peso.
7. South Africa is having a pilot run for Khokha.
8. Ghana is doing a pilot run for E-Cedi.
9. France has launched a pilot for France CBDC.

FEAR OF DISINTERMEDIATION BY BANKS

Commercial banks are concerned that CBDC would lead to the disintermediation of banks. Given an option, people will divert their deposits from banks to CBDC wallets. Loss of deposits can have a massive impact on the banking sector. Large-scale bank runs are

3 Bech and Garratt, 'Central Bank Cryptocurrencies'.
4 Ibid.
5 CBDC Tracker, 'Today's Central Bank Digital Currencies Status', n.d., https://cbdctracker.org/

likely to happen in the time of recession. Countries planning for CBDC need to address such concerns.

CHINA'S e-CNY

China's pilot CBDC, called e-CNY, now has 261 million users with $14 billion of transactions done already. E-CNY white paper claims it to be a 'digital currency with a difference' and the 'only fully regulated cryptocurrency, 100% backed by the Chinese government'. The white paper also states that e-CNY is 'the legal tender of world's second-largest economy. The currency is created on top of Binance smart chain, an open-source blockchain. Its official website allows other cryptocurrencies to be exchanged for e-CNY.[6]

Binance coin is the native token of the Binance smart chain. The claim of e-CNY being a cryptocurrency is a little incorrect. Since it is built on the top of the Binance chain, it is more like a crypto token.

The white paper states, 'The central bank will not compete with commercial banks.' China has set up a three-tier distribution system to avert the disintermediation of banks. Central banks will distribute the tokens to commercial banks; commercial banks will dispense the tokens to a middle custodian company. The custodian company will issue the tokens in the Binance smart chain and get them to the customers.

THE BAHAMAS'S SAND DOLLAR

The Bahamas was the first country to issue its CBDC. Sand dollar was launched in 2020. Its official website clearly states, 'Sand dollar is not a cryptocurrency.' Users will maintain a deposit account

6 Coco Feng, 'China's Digital Currency: e-CNY Wallet Nearly Doubles User Base in Two Months to 261 Million Ahead of Winter Olympics', 19 January 2022, https://www.scmp.com/tech/tech-trends/article/3163953/chinas-digital-currency-e-cny-wallet-nearly-doubles-user-base-two; https://ecnydigitalyuan.com/wp-content/uploads/2021/05/digitalyuan_ecny_whitepaper.pdf

with the central bank, allowing them to hold central bank liability. The Central bank of The Bahamas will issue sand dollars through authorized financial institutions or AFIs. It is a digital version of the Bahamian dollar, fully centralized, regulated and stable. It provides instantaneous validation of transactions, point of sale support for merchants, non-anonymous audit trail of transactions, fraud detection and digital ID solutions through KYC verification. Sand dollar's use is restricted for domestic use, unlike the Chinese e-CNY, which persuades others to invest in it.[7]

7 Digital Bahamian Dollar, https://www.sanddollar.bs/

26 WALLETS AND EXCHANGES

If you want to buy or sell cryptos or invest or trade, you should know how wallets and exchanges work. A wallet refers to a device which keeps track of your keys. It can be as simple as a piece of paper or as complex as computer hardware. You can imagine a wallet as a keychain. Currencies are locked up with your address in the blockchain. You must use your private key to unlock and spend them. You can own as many wallets you want as you can own several bank accounts.

EVOLUTION OF WALLETS

Satoshi Nakamoto suggested using different addresses each time you transact in bitcoin to ensure privacy. But generating a public–private key pair each time and securing them was tedious. Similarly, it was difficult to memorize a lengthy alphanumeric private key. Several BIPs were implemented to overcome these shortcomings.

BIP 32

The initial version of Bitcoin Core software came with a wallet. This wallet could generate a public–private key pair whenever you wanted. However, these pairs were not linked to each other. Hence, you had to back up each pair separately. Such wallets are called non-deterministic wallets, as there is no logical connection between various key pairs you own. In 2013, BIP 32 was implemented to create hierarchical deterministic wallets. These wallets could create a chain of addresses and private keys using a random number called a seed. The seed generates a single extended private key (xprv) called the master private key. The master key is then used to create child public–private key pairs, which generate their child keys. The key generation structure looks like a family tree. Every key pair is connected to the seed. Therefore, you can recover all your key pairs by backing up the seed. Further, BIP 32 enabled watch-only wallets, which helps you to receive and track funds without using your private key.

BIP 39

The seed was still hard to remember as it was a string of alphanumeric characters. BIP 39 introduced human-readable mnemonic seeds which could be used to recover all your keys. Following is an example of mnemonic seeds:

Train dust school wise cool tree tomato cattle furry book know horse

BIP 39 also allowed the user to add a passphrase during the key generation. A passphrase can be a word, number, sentence or a mix of all these. It provided an additional layer of security to the seeds. Even if someone gets hold of your seeds, they can't steal your coins unless they have the passphrase. Therefore, passphrases can be thought of as two-factor authentication.

BIP 44

'Multi-account hierarchy of deterministic wallets' was launched after BIP 44. It provided the flexibility to hold multiple coins with a single string of mnemonic words.

TYPES OF WALLETS

There are various types of wallets available. You should carefully go through the pros and cons before selecting a wallet.

Hot Wallets

Hot wallets are connected to the Internet, which makes fund transfer easy. Since the key pairs are stored in a web-based application, these are prone to cyberattacks. Therefore, you shouldn't keep large sums of money in hot wallets.

Cold Wallets

These wallets store the keys offline. You can use pieces of paper or metal to note down the key pairs. Cold wallets are the best wallets to store vast sums of cryptocurrency. Most users use third-party software to generate key pairs and note them down somewhere. When you use software written by others, you trust that they have used correct codes and not tracked your keys through hidden algorithms. Therefore, to create a truly cold wallet, you must pick up a notebook and do the ECDSA math to arrive at key pairs, or you should write the software to do the job. Large cryptocurrency companies store most of their holdings in cold wallets. However, creating and maintaining a cold wallet is arduous for a general user. The drawbacks of these wallets are that you can store only one key pair, and your money is gone if you forget the keys. Further, the physical object where the keys are written can be stolen, destroyed or lost.

Web Wallets

These wallets are hosted on a third-party website and accessed through a web browser. All web wallets are hot wallets and prone to online security issues. Most of these wallets are offered by cryptocurrency exchanges such as Coinbase and Binance. These are easy to use, as the exchange does the key management. You need not worry about forgetting the seed phrases or private keys, as the company will store them on your behalf. You need to create a user ID and a password. To activate the account, you must provide a KYC. You can always recover the password by using forget password option.

Such wallets are called 'custodial wallets', as the custody of keys lies with a third party. There is a massive risk of holding large amounts in custodial wallets because their servers can be hacked, or they can run away with your money. One such incident happened in 2014, when Mt. Gox, one of the largest bitcoin exchanges, was hacked. Around 850,000 bitcoins were stolen from the user wallets maintained by the exchange. There is speculation that the exchange itself might have carried out the theft.[1] Further, the private information in the KYC makes all your transactions traceable to you.

However, not all web wallets are custodial wallets. Some of these wallets provide control over your keys. The responsibility of safekeeping the seed phrase lies with you. If you lose the seed, you lose access to your money, and even the wallet provider cannot help you to recover. Such wallets are called 'non-custodial wallets'. For example, the wallet provided by blockchain.com is one of the oldest non-custodial web wallets available.

Mobile Wallets

These wallets are hot wallets which are available as Android and IOS apps. Most of the exchanges provide you app version of their web wallet. Hence, these apps suffer from the same drawbacks

1 Ben McLannahan, 'Bitcoin Exchange Mt Gox Files for Bankruptcy Protection', *Financial Times*, 28 February 2014, https://www.ft.com/content/6636e0e8-a06e-11e3-a72c-00144feab7de#axzz2v8woy2mI; Klint Finley, 'Bitcoin Exchange Mt. Gox Files for U.S. Bankruptcy as Death Spiral Continues', *Wired*, 10 March 2014, https://www.wired.com/2014/03/gox-texas/; Takashi Mochizuki, 'Japanese Police Arrest Mark Karpelès of Collapsed Bitcoin Exchange Mt. Gox', 1 August 2015, https://www.wsj.com/articles/japanese-police-arrest-mark-karpeles-of-collapsed-bitcoin-exchange-mt-gox-1438393669

as their web counterpart. Some apps are non-custodial and open source. These are comparatively more secure than the custodial mobile wallets.

Examples: Trust Wallet and MetaMask

Desktop Wallets

Such wallets run on Windows, Mac or Linux platforms. For example, Electrum and MetaMask are popular non-custodial desktop wallets used for Bitcoin and Ethereum, respectively.

Hardware Wallets

These are specialized devices used for storing cryptos. Keys are stored within the hardware. We can call these warm wallets, as these are connected to the Internet from time to time to carry out transactions. Hardware wallets are non-custodial, which makes them secure for storing large amounts. Ledger, KeepKey and Trezor are examples of popular hardware wallets.

Multi-signature Wallets

These are commonly referred to as multi-sig wallets. You can use both software and hardware to implement multi-sig wallets. These wallets need multiple private keys to authenticate transactions. One or more persons can hold keys. These are generally used by business partners who control a single wallet for the firm.

Backup and Recovery

Whenever you use a non-custodial wallet, you need to plan the backup and recovery of mnemonic seeds. You will receive a series of words while setting up a wallet. You must keep these carefully, as losing them means losing all your crypto money.

Some best practices to follow are as follows:

1. There can be 12–24 words. You must note them with correct spelling and order.
2. Write in ink that doesn't fade with time. Use good-quality paper. It's better if you laminate it.
3. Store the paper in a fireproof, tamper-resistant locker.
4. You can use a metal piece to inscribe the words. Make sure that the metal isn't prone to corrosion or humidity. Keep the metal wallet in a safe place.
5. Your wallet software may have a provision to test your backup later. Please make use of it.
6. Never share your seeds with anyone. Don't share personal information in response to an unverified message or mail.
7. If you use a web wallet, it will ask you for two-factor verification. It is better to use authenticator apps such as Google Authenticator and Authy, rather than SMS.

As long as you have the backup seeds, you can recover the cryptocurrencies even if your mobile, laptop or hardware wallet is destroyed or lost.

EXCHANGES

Exchanges are marketplaces for buying and selling cryptocurrencies. The price of currencies is decided by demand and supply. There are two types of exchanges.

Custodial Exchanges

These exchanges are *companies* which take custody of funds and permit you to trade on their platform. They will ask you to fill out a KYC form as per the anti-money-laundering regulations.

Merits

- They will manage the keys on behalf of you.
- You are free from the burden of backing up the keys.
- You can easily buy and sell cryptocurrencies.
- You can take benefit from various other services they provide. Most exchanges allow you to lock your cryptocurrencies for a fixed period to earn interest. This is called staking.
- Most of them allow P2P exchange of cryptos without fees.

Demerits

- You don't control your wallet.
- Exchanges are the single point of failure. You can lose money because of hacking, fraud, server failure, etc.
- All your transactions can be traced back to you. There is no anonymity.
- Private information provided during the KYC can be compromised and misused.
- They charge fees for every transaction done on their platform.

Non-custodial Exchanges

These are also called decentralized exchanges governed by smart contracts.

Merits

- They let you control your keys.
- You own your wallet.
- Many of them don't ask for KYC.
- They are more secure compared to custodial exchanges.

Demerits

- If you lose the key, you lose money.

- These are *crypto-only exchanges*. Therefore, you cannot convert your cryptos to fiat and vice versa.
- Many facilities of custodial exchanges are not available.

Checklist before You Select an Exchange

1. Study its reputation. Go through customer reviews online. You should check reviews in app store and play store.
2. Join Facebook and Telegram groups. Check the Twitter handle of the exchange. Try to gather opinions and experiences of people with the exchange. You will know which ones have poor customer service and shabby track records. Avoid such exchanges.
3. Keep a small amount of money in the exchange, and experience the platform for a month.
4. No matter how reputed the exchange, never hold a large sum of money in custodial exchange wallets.
5. Other factors to consider are fees, whether fiat withdrawal and deposit are permitted or not, response time of customer service, ease of use and kind of regulation it is subjected to.

27 REGULATIONS

This chapter will discuss the current status of cryptocurrency regulation worldwide. Suppose you are planning to invest in cryptos, create a cryptocurrency start-up or incorporate cryptos into your existing business. In that case, you must be aware of the regulatory environment. Laws can impact your business and investment decisions heavily.

The Library of Congress, USA, provides an excellent framework to study the crypto environment.[1] It identifies four legal states. Countries could be in one or more of such legal states concerning cryptocurrencies. These states are as follows.

Complete ban: This is the explicit ban carried out by law.
Implicit ban: Some countries may not have framed the laws to ban cryptocurrencies. However, they might have asked banks and financial institutions to refrain from dealing in cryptocurrencies or supporting individuals/companies that deal in cryptos.
Application of tax laws: If tax laws are applicable, cryptocurrency transactions within the country are taxed.
Application of Anti-money Laundering and Countering the Financing of Terrorism (AML/CFT) Laws: These laws,

1 Law Library of Congress, 'Regulation of Cryptocurrency around the World', 2021, https://www.loc.gov/item/2021687419/

if applied, bring cryptocurrency activities under strict monitoring. Crypto exchanges collect KYC because of the applicability of these laws.

As per the LOC, 9 countries have banned cryptocurrencies absolutely, and 42 countries have implemented implicit bans. One hundred and three countries have applied tax and AML/CFT to cryptocurrency. In addition to these, there can be other laws applicable to cryptocurrencies depending on the countries' regulatory environment.

El Salvador is the first country to legalize bitcoin. It passed the Bitcoin Law in June 2021, providing bitcoin with legal tender status within the country. Bitcoin transactions are subjected to tax under the Bitcoin Law. Further, the AML/CFT regulations are applicable.

In the case of the USA, there is no explicit or implicit ban on cryptos. Cryptocurrencies are treated as property by IRS for taxation. Anti-money laundering, Financial Crimes Enforcement Network and Combating the Financing of Terrorism Act applies to cryptocurrency exchanges. Crypto exchanges are also subjected to regulations under the Bank Secrecy Act.

Coming to China, it has taken an aggressive approach to curb cryptocurrency activity. It has implemented an absolute ban on cryptocurrencies. Binance, the world's largest cryptocurrency exchange, was forced to relocate to the Cayman Islands in 2017 after the People's Bank of China banned crypto exchanges. China is the largest hub for bitcoin miners because of its cheap electricity cost. However, it banned bitcoin mining in May 2021.[2] China doesn't provide details about the applicability of tax and AML to cryptocurrencies. Pakistan has an implicit ban on cryptocurrencies.

2 Bloomberg, 'China Urged to Close Loopholes in Crypto Mining Ban', 25 December 2021, https://www.bloomberg.com/news/articles/2021-12-25/china-must-close-loopholes-in-crypto-mining-ban-economic-daily

No information on taxability of crypto transaction is available. AML/CFT do not apply to cryptocurrencies in Pakistan.

In case of the UK, there is no explicit or implicit ban on cryptocurrencies. It has designed an elaborate taxation framework for individuals and companies dealing with cryptocurrencies. For example, individuals who hold cryptocurrencies for capital appreciation are liable to pay capital gain tax while disposing of the assets. If they run a trading business of cryptocurrencies, trading profits are taxable. There are separate provisions for business entities. Further, the Money Laundering, Terrorist Financing and Transfer of Funds Regulation, 2017, and Money Laundering and Terrorist Financing (Amendment) Regulation, 2019, apply to cryptos.

India's stance on cryptocurrencies until now is somehow negative. The Reserve Bank of India (RBI) banned cryptocurrencies in 2016. Later, in March 2020, the Supreme Court of India reversed the ban. Presently, there is no explicit or implicit ban on cryptocurrencies in India. The Cryptocurrency and Regulation of Official Digital Currency Bill, 2021, was listed for discussion in the winter session of the Parliament. The Bill aimed to create a framework for official digital currency issued by RBI. It also mentioned 'to prohibit all private cryptocurrencies' in India, which sparked speculations about what constitutes 'private cryptocurrencies'. Experts were divided into two groups: The optimistic group believed that private cryptos mean the so-called privacy currencies such as Monero and Dash, which completely obscure transaction details. If this is the case, bitcoin and other cryptocurrencies traded in a transparent and public blockchain will likely be out of the blanket ban. On the contrary, the pessimistic group couldn't ignore an older draft Bill called 'Banning of Cryptocurrency & Regulation of Official Digital Currency Bill, 2019'. This Bill has proposed severe punishment for anyone indulging in mining, buying, holding, selling and dealing in *cryptocurrencies*. Therefore, any cryptocurrency that RBI does not issue will be classified as a private cryptocurrency. This means that all cryptocurrencies will be banned. Indian crypto exchanges crashed following the confusion created by the Bill. Small investors lost a substantial amount of money.[3] However, the Bill wasn't tabled in the winter session. At present, it is under further development. The Government of India has implemented a massive 30 per cent tax on gains from crypto trading, which is at par with gains from betting on a horse race, winning the lottery, etc.

Regulations governing AML/CFT, Prevention of Money Laundering Act and relevant provisions under the Foreign Exchange Management Act are applicable to cryptocurrencies. Although RBI and the Indian government perceive cryptocurrencies as a threat to the country's economic stability, they are keen to explore use cases of blockchain technology. The Ministry of Electronics & Information Technology (MeitY) has formulated a national strategy on blockchain and the recent updated copy states its vision as follows:

> To create trusted digital platforms through shared Blockchain infrastructure; promoting research and development, innovation, technology and application development; and facilitating state of the art, transparent, secure and trusted digital service delivery to citizens and businesses, thus making India a global leader in Blockchain Technology.[4]

Recently, Maharashtra, one of the largest states in India, has decided to use Ethereum blockchain to secure educational certificates.[5] Further, RBI is determined to launch its CBDC called digital rupee soon.

3 Debangana Ghosh, 'Fearing Ban, Crypto Prices Crash', 24 November 2021, https://www.thehindubusinessline.com/economy/policy/cryptocurrencies-prices-drop-in-india-after-centre-moves-bill/article37656650.ece

4 Ministry of Electronics & Information Technology, *National Strategy on Blockchain* (December 2021), https://www.meity.gov.in/writereaddata/files/National_BCT_Strategy.pdf

5 DQIndia Online, 'Maharashtra to Use Ethereum Blockchain to Verify Diploma Certificates', 30 July 2021, https://www.dqindia.com/maharashtra-use-ethereum-blockchain-verify-diploma-certificates/

About the Author

Shubhasish Das is a finance professional and blockchain expert. He has over a decade of experience in the financial sector with different companies, including IBM, Philips, Maersk, Petrofac and Cargill. He is also an EdTech innovator and has created educational apps for the benefit of commerce students. His book *Think like an Accountant* is an Amazon India bestseller. Academically, he is a cost and management accountant from Institute of Chartered Accountants of India (ICAI), an affiliate member of Chartered Institute of Public Finance and Accountancy (CIPFA), a certified blockchain expert and a certified bitcoin professional. He is also a guest speaker at World Digital Weeks and a member of European Digital Experts Association.

STAY CONNECTED

Web: http://shubhasishdas.com/

Mail: mail@shubhasishdas.com

LinkedIn: https://www.linkedin.com/in/shubhasish-das-5a7385a7/

Instagram: das_shubhasish1

YouTube: Cryptos (https://www.youtube.com/channel/UC_ZiH1kyehu0KF2mC7-tF7A/featured)

EDUCATIONAL INVENTIONS

SIMPLEJE™ available on Google Play

Accounting Game available on Google Play